I0142381

TREASURES OF
REDEMPTION
The Key of Water Baptism!

Saheed Ogunsola

TREASURES OF REDEMPTION- The Key of Water Baptism
Copyright©2018 by Saheed Ogunsola.

All rights reserved. No portion of this book may be reproduced, stored in a
retrieval system, or transmitted in any form, or by any means - electronic,
mechanical, photocopy, recording, scanning, or other without the prior writte
permission of the author.

Request for information on this title should be addressed to
Saheed Ogunsola
RCCG Grace Pavilion Parish,
Lakowe Lakes Golf Road,
Lakowe, Ibeju-Lekki, Lagos, Nigeria.
Email: upwords247@gmail.com
+234 816 898 3785

Unless otherwise indicated, all scripture quotations are from the Holy Bible: Ki
James Version (KJV). All Rights Reserved.

First Published in Nigeria, 2016, by Sherib Limited, Lagos, Nigeria

Library of Congress Cataloging-in-Publication Data

Saheed Ogunsola
TREASURES OF REDEMPTION- The Key of Water Baptism
ISBN-13: 978-1-946530-13-4 (Paperback)
ISBN-10: 1-946530-13-1 (Paperback)
1. Inspiration - Non-fiction 1. Title
Library of Congress Control Number: 2018951739

Designed by Sherib

Published in Dallas Texas by Pyxidia House Publishers. A registered trademark
Pyxidia Concept llc. www.pyxidiahouse.com info@pyxidiahouse.com

Printed in the United States of America

Table of Contents

FOREWORD

The Bible clearly teaches that baptism is the first step of obedience after making a commitment to Christ. Baptism allows believers to communicate to the world their heart-felt commitment to Christ.

Baptism by full immersion as taught in the Bible, is an act of obedience that should be an immediate part of our acceptance of the gift of grace offered by Jesus Christ. It illustrates Christ's death, burial and resurrection.

"For what I received I passed on to you as of first importance: that Christ died for our sins according to the Scriptures, that he was buried, that he was raised on the third day..."(1 Corinthians 15:3-4).

As rightly put by Pastor Saheed Ogunsola, "water baptism has pointed us to the immerse work of redemption in Christ and the change of citizenship that follows for every believer and receiver of the grace of salvation that is in Him".

When we understand this perspective, the insight and thoughtfulness of Pastor Saheed Ogunsola will be appreciated.

Likewise, the expediency of immersion in water (for all born again children of God) as it symbolizes not only death and purification, but also regeneration and renewal will be treasured.

The principal effects of water baptism are: purification from sins, and new birth in the Holy Spirit.

Treasures of Redemption encapsulates baptism as a wedding ring; the outward symbol of the commitment we made in our heart that has to be followed through and lived out on a daily basis.

This work is an eye opener to rekindle, renew and reaffirm God's purpose for human race. It is recommended to all who are eager to reclaim their spiritual inheritance, a must read for all serious and righteous minded believers.

I pray that this book will help shed more light on your decision to follow in the footsteps of Jesus Christ, our Lord and Saviour.

Pastor Sola Agunbiade
Pastor-In-Charge
RCCG Lagos Province 23.

ENDORSEMENTS

"It is with great pleasure that I recommend this excellent book by Pastor Saheed Ogunsola. This book examines the treasures of redemption and specifically the treasure of water baptism, a divine blessing that even our Lord Jesus Christ partook of. This book reveals the significance, inherent power and blessings attached to this godly ordinance. I recommend this book for the enlightenment and edification of every believer.

Pastor (Mrs) Oluwatoyin Sanni
Group CEO, United Capital PLC
Pastor, Author, Banker, Entrepreneur & Int'l Speaker

"This book is indeed a treasure as it gives further insight on the deep blessings embedded in water baptism. It opens up a well of knowledge from a deeper understanding of the spiritual implication of water baptism. For those coming from a different spiritual background like me, it explains the critical importance of the event with experiential knowledge. This book is therefore highly recommended for every Christian."

Deacon Biodun Oyapero
Financial Expert & Investor,
MD / CEO First Capital Trust Limited

"I had the rare privilege of having an electronic copy of this book before it hit the prints. This book is a refreshingly positive exposition on baptisms and a true picture of the treasures of our redemption! I gladly recommend it to all."

Rev. Victor Ayodele
Pastor, Church of God Mission Int'l
Katy, Texas, USA

TREASURES OF REDEMPTION an insightful piece loaded with Revelation and information that brings about irrecoverable spiritual Revolution. In these writings the mystery of redemption is unveiled with ease of understanding. reading through the pages added value to my knowledge of the essence of redemption.

Pastor Saheed has been used by The Lord to put these exegesis in black and white. I recommend this book to Believers who want more understanding of Jesus' mission on earth.
In addition I strongly believe it is a tool for Evangelism. As you read may you be richly blessed in Jesus' name.

Evangelist 'Gboyega Shitta
President, Kingdom Power Ministries Int'l
Manchester, UK

A master stroke that reveals yet another mystery of our Faith. This book has uncovered deeper revelations about baptism not just to unbelieving "believers" but to those who before now may assume to know everything about the teachings on baptism.

Treasures of Redemption is a pointer that every one has the opportunity to tap into the realm of unlimited access to God through Jesus Christ only when you continually seek to know more and believe Him.

Thanks to the author for this unspeakable gift.

Pastor Timothy Aliyeju Mordi
R.C.C.G Missionary Pastor (Europe)

ACKNOWLEDGMENT

Life is built on relationships. You never succeed alone. No man is self-made. Written all over creation is the power of influence through relationships. The sun, moon and stars influence happenings on the earth.

First and foremost is the Lord God Almighty, Jehovah Adonai, the Lord whose name is too great to be called anyhow. I am very thankful for His mercies and goodness over my life. His love is still beyond my comprehension. To The Lord Jesus Christ, who left all to search for me, found and saved me. To the Holy Spirit, by whom life came into these dead and dry bones, thank You!

Whether in the immediate or remote, there are men and women, who over the years have been used of God to influence and mold our lives. We may not be able to mention them all, but there are few who represent the rest.

To my biological dad, Deacon Riliwan Aremu Ogunsola, I am very thankful. To Deaconess Moteleola Abake Ogunsola, my biological mother, I am equally full of thanks, and to all my brothers and sisters.

To the spiritual fathers the Lord God setup ahead of us as His beacons of light, Pastor E.A. Adeboye, Bishop David Oyedepo, Kenneth Copeland, and a host of others, may the river of life keep flowing and the nations be delivered and healed. I am very thankful to God for the life of Austin T. Sparks.

As an under-shepherd in the Redeemed Christian Church of God (RCCG) myself, there are many mentors the Lord has used and is still using to raise us up. A few of which are Pastor J.T. Odesola, Pastor Brown Oyitso, Pastor Femi Olawale (Canada), Pastor Funsho Adedayo, Pastor J.T. Kalejaiye, Pastor Austin Ukaiwe, Pastor Sola Agunbiade, just to mention a few among a host of other most senior pastors in the RCCG, I am very thankful for God's exceptional grace and blessing upon your lives.

Pastor Tonye Oliver (JHTS Ministries), HRM Sola Adedoyin-Alao, Evang. Shitta Gboyega (KPMI), God bless you immensely and keep you all.

Outstanding among many are: Pastor Femi Odugbemi, my mentor, and his precious wife, Jewel Regina Odugbemi, Pastor Bimbo Oresegun, an astounding man of God, special thanks to you all.

To "Mr. & Mrs. Smith" - Pastor Segun Lookman Sanni and his very precious wife and outstanding woman of God, Pastor (Mrs) Toyin Sanni, I love and owe you so much.

Lady Kehinde Kamson, Captain Owolabi Martins, Daddy Biodun Oyapero and his dear wife, Mummy Bola Oyapero, Mrs. Omolara Olaniran, Mr Olaniran Ogundipe and Mrs Chidi Essell – my precious Sister from another mother, I am indebtedly grateful to God for your faith in God toward me and your shining lives.

Bishop – Pastor Abidemi Adekoya, Pastor David Nwagu, Pastor Kola Fashola, Pastor Lolade Ojomo and a host of other PICs spread all over the RCCG, thank you for being partners in this great work. Standing with you all shoulder-to-shoulder in the Lord's vineyard is a great priviledge.

Every great athlete out there has a secret coach. Coaches are not always visible but they do great works in the hidden. To my God given coach, Pastor (Mrs) Morinsola Ogunsola – precious turtle dove, immense thanks. To my blessed and boisterous musketeers Jethro, Judah (Mishael) and Jemima, you are treasures beyond measure!

To all the family members of RCCG Goshen, Hephzibah and now, Grace Pavilion, you are greatly treasured. God bless you immensely more! Very special thanks to Deacon Biodun Akanni, Pastor Akin Morakinyo and wife, Tola Morakinyo. Deacon Emmanuel Ndaks, my precious son in the faith, Pastor Amadasu Enorense, Pastor (Dr.) Praise Akpunne, Pastor Chris Bako and families, you all are warmly acknowledged.

A/P Kunle Shokunbi and my precious doctor, Deaconess Funmi Shokunbi, Daddy Ayo Ifaturoti and his dear wife, Deaconess Seyi Ifaturoti, Emmanuel and Bunmi Orosun, thank you for being special to me.

Pastors Debola and Bunmi Ajaguna (Canada), you both, and the Lord's troop in your care are such a great blessing to me.

To the great team at RCCG Dove Media, RED media, especially my daughter, "shautish" Seun Anjorin, thank you for being great helpers in life!

Then came along my newest son Lawrence Iriferigoma, who took great pains to carefully go through the manuscripts and made so many corrections. Thank you for your immense contributions to this project.

If it seems you have not been mentioned by name, it's not because you are not important. You are heaven chosen and precious, Heaven acknowledges you and shall bless you exceeding more. Thank you for being a great blessing to my life!

DEDICATION

Mrs. Regina Odugbemi.
A woman of great faith!

PROLOGUE

Fulfilment Is Here!

"Your new self (which is Christ's & also yours) will not come as long as you are looking for it. It will come when you are looking for Him."

- CS Lewis

Prologue

"For all the prophets and the law prophesied until John."
– Matthew 11:13.

Apicture speaks a thousand words, so goes the saying. And how true it is! Much words are embedded within a picture – which captures not just images but time.

> *"The law and the prophets were until John: since that time the kingdom of God is preached, and every man presseth into it."*
> *– Luke 16:16.*

When John the baptizer arrived on the scene, the true picture of all that the prophets and laws had prophesied, foretold or represented began to take a solid form – fulfilment began.

We are well informed that the laws had shadows of things to come. And where there are shadows, light and images are around the corner. When Jesus Christ showed up, the true and perfect image of things began to manifest for all to see!

"For the law having a shadow of good things to come, and not the very image of the things, can never with those sacrifices which they offered year by year continually make the comers thereunto perfect."- Hebrews 10:1.

Even that which had been invisible, we began to see in and through Him. Jesus came as light to make things once hidden manifest! He is the image of the invisible God! (Colossians 1:15, Hebrews 1:3). All that had ever eluded man came to light in and through Him!

3

"Let no man therefore judge you in meat, or in drink, or in respect of an holyday, or of the new moon, or of the sabbath days: Which are a <u>shadow of things</u> to come; but <u>the body is of Christ.</u>" – Colossians 2:16-17.

The New Testament is like a picture, revealing what God had in mind when the men of old prophesied, and unveiling of the future altogether. It's a comprehensive thing. All of the past, present and the future have therefore found fulfilment and completion in Christ Jesus the Lord!

"Think not that I am come to destroy the law, or the prophets: I am not come to destroy, but to <u>fulfil</u>." – Matthew 5:17

You will discover that virtually every statement and action in the New Testament, most especially and essentially that of Christ is a summary of many details embedded in the Old Testament prophecies, laws and Psalms. So much history is gathered into every truth therein.

In the same vein, when Jesus Christ came, as a great teacher and one whose life and actions holds the explanation to everything, He taught with parables in detailing the Kingdom of God to man.

However, just as actions speak as much, if not louder than words, not all His parables were spoken. There were acted parables -practical demonstrations which were intended to help drive home His Kingdom teachings.

Water baptism is a vital act that holds or pieces together the past, present and future in God's plan of salvation for man.

4

As short as this ritual is, it embodies all the prophecies and promises ever made by God regarding man and creation in general! It is an act, mysteriously deep and full of power, brought to full light, among many things, in the New Testament by the manifest presence of the Redeemer (2 Timothy 1:10).

Now, water baptism – as a symbol or summary of the redemption works, takes only a few seconds to conduct, but it gathers a thousand things together at once! This is what this piece of write up is all about – just to have a glimpse of the things gathered up together in and through water baptism, and the things every believer stands to explore, discover and enjoy!

Those few seconds during the dip in the waters at water baptism represent the three days and three nights the Lord Jesus Christ spent in the deep or the belly of the earth at His death, as declared by Him and prophesied in Jonah. Also, what transpired in the Lord's conversation with John the Baptizer before being dipped in water, the mystery of what happened under the water and immediately after are some of the things we seek to briefly explore and discover.

This book seeks to help unfold as much as can be touched regarding this all important sacrament of water baptism that we may press further in the living knowledge of the Saviour and His work, walking and living in the better things that accompany His salvation.

There is so much about water baptism that the Orientals, even from and with diverse religious backgrounds don't handle with levity.

Dynamites may be small in size but no one can ignore their effects. The little shared in this book, by the help of the Holy Ghost, will surely revolutionize your life!

Welcome to change!

CHAPTER ONE

The Bridge of No Return!

*"What a tremendous amount we hear!
What a tremendous amount of information is given to
us! What a lot we know! Do we assume that, because
we have all that knowledge, we are really livingly
related to the Lord Jesus? The test is: What is the value
of our knowledge? Is there a sting in it? Is there a
living element in it? Is there effectiveness in it? Is it a
knowledge that is going through to accomplishment, to
reach the end? Is it, in a word, living knowledge?"*

- Austin Sparks

The Case for Rootedness!

"Forasmuch as many have taken in hand to set forth in order a declaration of those things which are most surely believed among us, Even as they delivered them unto us, which from the beginning were eyewitnesses, and ministers of the word; It seemed good to me also, having had perfect understanding of all things from the very first, to write unto thee in order, most excellent Theophilus, That thou mightest know the certainty of those things, wherein thou hast been instructed." – Luke 1:1-4.

There yet seem to be a general and persistent weakness in the lives of many people in the body of Christ today because there is lack of depth regarding some of the fundamentals of this great faith! The Christian life is a unique, uncommon life, foreign to this present world or age, and outstanding in every way. Yet, only few in the faith understand this uniqueness in its true depth. And more pathetic is the fact that only a few seek or desire to know.

> *"We have to be continually reminded of what we believe."*
> *- CS Lewis*

Many are thus living far below the best of what is laid up for them in God's redemption programme in and through Christ Jesus, the man of His right hand, the Lord and Saviour!

As it is written, it is evident that there is a form of godliness in many, but its dynamic power is largely lacking! (2 Timothy 3:5). This lack of knowledge has made many to become preys to jackals in sheep's skin!

8

As boldly stated in the preceding scripture by Doctor Luke centuries ago, it is very important to be certain or rooted in the things we have come to believe, as many believers have fallen short of experiencing the best their faith holds for them.

In his opening sentence in the Gospel Book of Luke, Luke the Physician mentioned that there are many firsthand eyewitnesses and minsters of word on whose accounts many have come to have faith in Jesus Christ. However, he has done a lot of research and investigative work on these things and he's therefore giving account unto this exalted man, Theophilus, so that his faith will be secure and grounded.

In the same vein, many have undertaken to write books on the faith of the believer, the richness and riches of redemption. Many authors have written from their personal experiences in order to spur, motivate or encourage others.

It seem good to me also by the grace of God, beloved, to write this short piece in order to help someone further and farther in this great journey of faith in Christ Jesus and the treasures of His redemption.

Definitely I am not perfect, and do not boast of having perfect understanding either but strongly believe, by the Spirit of Grace of the living God, that the depth of understanding shown me so far can help liberate others unto deeper, fuller joys of His redemption!

Also, there is an account written by the same Doctor Luke in the book of Acts chapter 19 that reinforces the fact that a man may miss out in the riches of redemption if he is not well instructed. This classical case is still true in the lives of many believers or people of faith in the Lord Jesus Christ today.

Which or Whose Baptism?

"And it came to pass, that, while Apollos was at Corinth, Paul having passed through the upper coasts came to Ephesus: and finding certain disciples, He said unto them, Have ye received the Holy Ghost since ye believed?

And they said unto him, We have not so much as heard whether there be any Holy Ghost.

And he said unto them, Unto what then were ye baptized? And they said, Unto John's baptism.

Then said Paul, John verily baptized with the baptism of repentance, saying unto the people, that they should believe on him which should come after him, that is, on Christ Jesus. When they heard this, they were baptized in the name of the Lord Jesus.

And when Paul had laid his hands upon them, the Holy Ghost came on them; and they spake with tongues, and prophesied. And all the men were about twelve."
– Acts 19:1-7.

Beloved, how shall they believe in Him whom they have never heard? How shall they act and receive the promised blessings without faith? (Romans 10:14).

The men in this scripture were disciples – adherent learners, and not just casual believers. These were dedicated men who were not taking lightly their new found faith and life. Yet, there were essential things they lacked in instructions which could have taken them to another level in their walk of faith! Apostle Paul must have perceived the fragrance of the Holy Ghost missing in these lives, and therefore enquired after Him in their lives.

We have many "lifeless" Christians like these men today in whose lives the promised abundant life is not manifesting, and the fragrance of Christ's knowledge is missing! (John 10:10).

> *"Now thanks be unto God, which always causeth us to triumph in Christ, and maketh manifest the savour of his knowledge by us in every place."*
> *-2Cor. 2:14.*

With these disciples, John the Baptizer had done the first part of the process of cleansing with water, which Apostle Paul referred to as baptism unto repentance, but they needed to move to the next level which is the Holy Spirit for the greater life!

However, they *"...have not so much as heard whether there be any Holy Ghost"* So, how will they come into the abundant life without Him? How will they enjoy the better things that accompany Christ's salvation?

We must press on in the knowledge of our faith as ignorance is a great threat and arrester in this journey of life! (Isaiah 5:13). We are baptized into and unto the Son of God at salvation but there is another baptism that empowers and makes us His living witnesses.

11

From this account in Acts chapter 19, we have people who are in the faith but are not instructed on the person of the Holy Spirit. Their number being 12 may not be a coincidence at all. Twelve is a spiritual number of government, rulership or administration. Their number implies there could be a crop of the Lord's people, men under His government, people of faith, who are still not in the know of further things that redemption in Christ holds for them. They live good lives but are limited by the reason of the absence of knowledge or instruction in certain areas.

The Holy Ghost has already being given but these men were unaware of this divine provision. Blessed be God for when knowledge came, they believed, they did the needful and captivity ended! They could now go farther than ever in the faith – they spoke the heavenly language and prophesied! These men keyed into the heavenlies with the Holy Ghost and things began to happen in them, and I believe, through them.

The same can be yours when the entrance of the word happens in your heart! The light of His life ensues and darkness gets dispelled!

This little book is written *"That thou mightest know the certainty of those things, wherein thou hast been instructed"*, and then go on to enjoy what Christ has wrought and laid up for us as our heritage (Acts 20:32).

When I also came into the light and certainty of the things I had believed, it changed the game for me, my life was freshly transformed. However, it took people outside Christ or

12

Christianity to make me know the depth of what I had come into in Christ. Since then, I am still digging and finding treasures in the inexhaustible Life of the Lord and Saviour – Jesus Christ!

"...But they regard not the work of the LORD, neither consider the operation of his hands. Therefore my people are gone into captivity, because they have no knowledge: and their honourable men are famished, and their multitude dried up with thirst." – Isaiah 5:12-13.

There are those dying of thirst and lack in the ocean of plenty. Don't be part of them! By the light of Christ's knowledge, every manner of captivity or limitation ends in your life today! This is the accepted time, and the day of your liberation!

Divine Interpreters

"And Philip ran thither to him, and heard him read the prophet Esaias, and said, Understandest thou what thou readest? And he said, How can I, except some man should guide me? And he desired Philip that he would come up and sit with him."
- Acts 8:30.

There are things we read from scriptures and except we have God sent interpreters, it will be struggles all the way for us. When Philip, by the Holy Ghost, starting from the same scripture opened up everything to the Ethiopian Eunuch, his life changed. He never returned to Africa the same man!

"If there be a messenger with him, an interpreter, one among a thousand, to shew unto man his uprightness: Then he is gracious

unto him, and saith, Deliver him from going down to the pit: I have found a ransom. His flesh shall be fresher than a child's: he shall return to the days of his youth." – Job 33:23-25.

Many of the arrest we still see in the lives of believers today is a function of the lack of revelation knowledge. And there are many wolves today in sheep's skin taking advantage of this ignorance and therefore devouring many. You shall not be their victim!

It is strongly believed that the refreshingness from the breath of God that inspired this little book shall bring about undeniable changes or transformations in your own life! This is why God raises shepherds after His own heart who will feed the flock with knowledge and understanding.

My Case - The Bridge of No Return

Like all men, I was not born a Christian. And the truth is: no man is ever born a Christian! It's simply not possible with man. Salvation in Christ is non-transferable! People may be born into Christianity, but no one is ever born a Christian. It's an act solely carried out by God upon those who believe and receive His Son Jesus Christ as their Lord and Saviour.

That Jesus Christ was born in a manger never made Him an animal just like living in a garage never makes you a vehicle! So, being born into a Christian home never automatically makes you a Christian. Until you are born again, you are not a Christian. Period!

While studying in the university, I saw different crops of Christians. Some were happy, inwardly and outwardly but some were simply outwardly sad. And you know that your inward experience determines your outward manifestation!

However, priviledged by God, I "saw" or discerned some of these Christians as people who had possession without understanding. I strongly sensed at that time that they had something of joy that many of them were not enjoying. They were supposed to be happy people but it never showed in some of them. Consciously or unconsciously, I prayed that one day, in case I ever become a Christian, God should not make me like the majority of these Christians who carried sad countenances.

In summary, on a fateful Saturday evening in October, 1990, in the course of a very brief and deep encounter with God, I gave my life to Jesus Christ. Kneeling on my bed in my room located in the L-Block of the Male hostel of the Federal University of Technology (FUT) Minna, all alone, I received Jesus Christ as my Lord and Saviour! It's a day that continues to linger forever!

It was swift and electric, and the impression it left, by God's grace, can never be erased! I became born again! I became a new man, and I knew it! Though I was ignorant of the protocol of being born again, I knew I had become a Christian after that encounter with Jehovah God! He took me in as His own just as I was! Heaven was aglow for me that fateful and unforgettable day!

The following morning, Sister Irene Atenega (of blessed memory who later became Mrs. Irene Jide-Crown) came visiting after her church service and as we met by the door way of my hostel, I informed her that I am now a Christian! She never paused or hesitated to ask how I got born again but dragged me straight to her church and pastor –Rev. Andrew Agbein, the then resident pastor of Evangelical Christian Fellowship (ECF) situated in Bosso town of Minna, Niger state, Nigeria.

Beloved, that was how my journey of faith in Jesus Christ began, in October 1990!

All along the way, after many people got wind of my conversion, there was anger and resentment from the people of my former religion. But our God knows how to take charge of things. My case was simply different!

In the course of my journey, I got close to the then Vice Chancellor's wife who was working on her PhD thesis and needed a proficient computer user for the work. That was how I was recommended for her work as everyone knew my proficiency with computer back then in FUT Minna.

She made every effort as any compassionate mother would, to lure or bring me back to Islam but those efforts didn't work. My conversion was not with the help of any man, and no man was going to drag me back! We often had arguments at times and there were occasions she ordered me out of her office or sight. However, I knew it was out of love and therefore did not take offence.

Then one day, while sitting opposite her she looked at me with a strange glance, and I asked why she did so. In fact, I sent the first arrow to remind her that she was going to start religious talks, argument and fights again but she shocked me with her response.

She informed me that "they" have instructed her not to try to convert me back to Islam. Now that response jostled me, that there were people she had been consulting with on my case. However, what they told her troubled me more even though it became a thing of endless joy later.

Looking at me straight in the eye she said that she had been informed I had **"crossed the bridge of no return!"** And that it will be useless trying to get me back.

While I was happy that no man will be pursuing me again, I asked her what they meant by the crossing of **"the bridge of no return."** Her response was deeply shocking and troubling!

"Acts 4:16 – Through [the] centuries, the enemy has woefully failed at discrediting Christ's resurrection as inexplicable miracles have testified to His [grace and] Name! Yours is next! -Acts 1:8"
- Saheed Ogunsola

She was told I had done water baptism! And because of the water baptism that I had done, I am lost to them **forever**! It was of no use pursuing who doesn't exist! No one continues to converse with a dead man!

Now, I never informed anyone that I was going to do water baptism or that I had done water baptism. How "the people" knew I had done water baptism is still a puzzle till date. But I remember the case of Laban and Jacob in scriptures.

17

"And Laban said unto him, I pray thee, if I have found favour in thine eyes, tarry: for I have learned by experience that the LORD hath blessed me for thy sake." – Genesis 30:27.

The word translated **"experience"** in this scripture means divination, enchantment or spell. Laban, by divination, discovered things about Jacob. That must have been my case too!

These people who said I had **"crossed the bridge of no return"** informed her that **"the man who came out of the water during baptism wasn't the same man who went inside."** The man in the water was forever lost to them and the man out of the water is a new creature, of a new nature and nation.

They gave up the pursuit! I pray for you that in the like manner, by your baptism into Christ, your pursuers shall give up on you too!

Now, those who taught me about water baptism never told me, instructed me nor gave me a very deep detail as these "outsiders" of the faith did. They seemed to understand more than those who taught me. They were outsiders of the Christian faith but understood the in-working of things.

Their explanation opened up a world of light in me and for me! My search for deeper understanding of what I have come to believe, the pursuit of my Saviour, has been unabated since!

When I returned home from school, and my mother was protesting about some observations about my Christian life, I informed my father to tell her that the boy they sent to school was not the one who returned.

This is another man! The statement came from my knowledge of what water baptism had opened up in the plan of redemption!

Believers therefore need to be well taught or instructed in the things of the Lord. There are too many shallow Christians who have become easy prey for wolves in sheep's clothing.

This book is about bringing you into the knowledge of the treasures of salvation for every believer as illustrated or symbolized through water baptism!

The Lord is going to use the key of water baptism to open the door of endless treasures of redemption Christ Jesus secured for us. They are yours to eternally live on!

As you go through this piece, may your life be richer than ever, may you rise higher than ever, be bolder than ever, be made greater and shine brighter than ever in the glory of God's amazing grace.

Welcome to newness!

CHAPTER TWO

The Beginning of the Gospel

"One cannot measure the Man of Galilee with any tape line or yardstick that comes from human reasoning.

Jesus [Christ] is outside that realm of reason."

-John G Lake

The Beginning of the Gospel

As we take steps to proceed in our discourse in this book, it is very pertinent to see the layout of the Lord's ministry and understand the place of water baptism – that is, what it stands for, and the works or blessings that follow. The Gospel Book of Mark helps so greatly in this regard.

> *"By the light of nature we see God as a God above us, by the light of the law, we see Him as a God against us, but by the light of the Gospel we see Him as Emmanuel, God with us!"*
> *- Matthew Henry*

The Book began introducing the focus of its content:

"The beginning of the gospel of Jesus Christ, the Son of God."
- Mark 1:1.

The Book is about the message of the ministry of Jesus Christ, the Son of God. Then, the writer, under the inspiration and direction of the Holy Spirit, showcased how His Gospel started.

The word translated **"Gospel"** is the Greek word "Euaggelion" or "Evangellion" which is a combination of two words: **"Eu"** meaning "Good" and **"Angelos"** meaning "Angel or Messenger". The entire word, in transliteration, therefore means **"Good Messenger"** which invariably implies **"Good news"**.

The Gospel is therefore generally accepted or referred to as the announcement of Good Message or Good News.

What Is Good News?

There is no ambiguity about the word **"Good"**. If something is good, then it is cheery, satisfactory, and brings pleasure or joy.

Now what is *"News"*?

We live in a dispensation wherein *"Breaking News"* has become an everyday phrase that, in fact, many look forward to. If we understand *"News"* from the Lord's perspective, it will surely revolutionize our lives. Our attitudes to His Gospel will never be the same again.

News is a report of a recent event, intelligence or information. It is the presentation of a report on recent or new events. It is an event or something of recent origin or production. News is something of a kind now existing or appearing for the first time, a novel. It is an event or information having being but lately coming into knowledge. These are dictionary meanings of news.

In summary, news, in a very basic or simple term, is the dissemination of information about an event that has recently taken place in order to make those unaware to be informed or aware.

An information given you is news when you have not heard it before or unaware of the information. What you hear is no more news when you already have known about the information or event.

News therefore brings you into the light of an event you are previously unaware of.

Then the writer of the Book of Mark informed us that:

"Now after that John was put in prison, Jesus came into Galilee, preaching the gospel of the kingdom of God, And saying, The time is fulfilled, and the kingdom of God is at hand: <u>repent ye, and believe the gospel</u>." – Mark 1:14-15.

Now, as written here, Christ's Gospel – the Good Message or Good News – is about **something that has recently happened** - what everyone needed to be aware of. **The fulfilling of time**, and the arrival of **the Kingdom of God or God's Sovereign rule!**

That **good thing** or **tiding** being proclaimed as having happened is what this book tries to explore. We need to understand what happened as our life under the government of the Holy Spirit depends on it. We cannot come to that promised abundant life if we are in the dark regarding the things fulfilled!

After hearing, Jesus says, we are to repent –change our mind and way of thinking, receive and act on the good news. It's that straight forward!

Now, before we are told what the gospel of Jesus Christ was or is, the author wrote of events between verses 2 and 14 which are the things the Good News is all about!

What happened therefore – the good events that brought the good news, is extremely important for us to know and understand in their depth. The activities of our Lord within these verses seem to be all that the whole creation had waited for and therefore got fulfilled! There are volumes of promises, prophecies through inspired men and the law, and eternal things connected with these events that worth all our attention.

Now, the summary or key event was **the manifestation of the Lamb of God,** whom no one knew, including John the Baptizer himself, but that He should be made manifest or brought to light or knowledge through John's ministry.

At His water baptism, there was witness from God, the Holy Spirit and John himself about the identity of Jesus Christ. And after His wilderness experience which followed immediately, which the Gospel Book of Mark did not bother to elaborate on, Jesus returned in the power of the Spirit and began to preach the Gospel of the Kingdom with signs and wonders following!

He received the witness for doing, all through His earthly life, what no man could do. His words and actions were those of an uncommon man who stood out among men! He was truly another man! Where all men failed, He succeeded. And all He did stemmed from His baptism. This is because the man who came out from the water was not of this world order or creation!

There is something therefore that makes every believer in Christ Jesus an uncommon man **for all in Him are made**

after His kind! May you henceforth, through your redemption status, stand out among others! The light and grace that made Him the fairest shall distinguish you too!

"Thou art fairer than the children of men: grace is poured into thy lips: therefore God hath blessed thee for ever." – Psalm 45:2.

Now, from the discourse in this great Gospel Book, the appearance of Jesus Christ, the Son of God marked the beginning of the end of John's ministry. John came as a forerunner to bring Him on the public stage and therefore bowed out after He was announced.

Now, other accounts of the Gospel gave us further details of what transpired with respect to the baptism and the wilderness experience. But the water baptism in Jordan, that took not more than a few seconds to perform, seemed to gather together all the fulfilment of times, prophecies and promises. An act of just a few seconds packed together all that has ever been promised and the opening of eternity.

Surely, there is so much to know and understand about that simple ritual of water baptism.

The Good News!

We need to understand better what the content of Lord's Gospel or message is.

"There is but on good, that is God. Everything else is good when it looks to Him and bad when it turns from Him." - CS Lewis

"And Jesus returned in the power of the Spirit into Galilee: and there went out a fame of him through all the region round about.

25

And he taught in their synagogues, being glorified of all. And he came to Nazareth, where he had been brought up: and, as his custom was, he went into the synagogue on the sabbath day, and stood up for to read. And there was delivered unto him the book of the prophet Esaias. And when he had opened the book, he found the place where it was written,

The Spirit of the Lord is upon me, because he hath anointed me to <u>preach the gospel</u> to the poor; he hath sent me to heal the brokenhearted, to <u>preach deliverance</u> to the captives, and recovering of sight to the blind, to set at liberty them that are bruised, to <u>preach</u> the acceptable year of the Lord.

And he closed the book, and he gave it again to the minister, and sat down. And the eyes of all them that were in the synagogue were fastened on him.

And he began to say unto them, This day is this scripture fulfilled in your ears." - Luke 4:14-21.

Now, after His wilderness experience in which the devil could not floor Him, Jesus returned to Galilee, this time, in the power of the Holy Spirit and began to preach the Gospel. This quoted scripture in Luke chapter 4 detailed for us the beginning of His Gospel.

Jesus declared that by the Holy Spirit resting upon Him, from His Jordan baptism, He has been anointed to preach – declare, proclaim, announce the Good News to the poor, announce deliverance to the captives, declare recovery of sight to the blind, proclaim the opening of prison...

His mission was about <u>declaring</u> what has been accomplished. That's the heart of His message —declaration! It wasn't about what will be done but **what has already happened!** There is something that HAS been done that the poor or the oppressed needed to know and enjoy, those in prison or captivity should know there is a good news about their case, also that those who are blind have a good news, and finally to make all men know what time they are in!

What had been a set of promises in the book of Isaiah, among other promises and prophecies, has been fulfilled and the people needed to know this and come into the good of it! The Lord's work was largely p r o c l a m a t i o n   o r announcement of what has happened that men needed to change their thinking about and embrace the news or act on His news, good news!

> *"Never lose heart in the power of the gospel.*
> *Do not believe that there exists any man, much less any race of men, for whom the gospel is not fitted."*
> *- Charles H. Spurgeon*

As far as the Lord was concerned, whatever may be the need of men, it has been met already!

Therefore, the poor does not have to remain poor again, the blind does not have to remain blind again, the captive or prisoner does not have to remain in captivity again and the bruised have healing already in place and they don't need to remain ever sick again! This is the Gospel, Christ's Gospel!

27

All His works that followed after His mission declaration - the miracles, healings, arising of the dead, are fruits or products of what had happened that He began to enforce in every believer or receiver of His word! Everything He did, which He also said believers would do after He has returned to the Father, are rooted in the things signified by His water baptism in Jordan and His wilderness experience or temptation!

All His works are the better things of life which follow His work of salvation!

"But, beloved, we are persuaded better things of you, and things that accompany salvation, though we thus speak."
– Hebrews 6:9 .

Beloved, make every effort, diligently immersing yourself in His word, to see and discover those things He accomplished so that you can live in the good of His works in a fuller way than ever!

"For we are his workmanship, created in Christ Jesus unto good works, which God hath before ordained that we should walk in them." – Ephesians 2:10.

Today forward, may you walk in the good works accomplished for you! By the power of the Holy Ghost, you shall be a living witness of His amazing grace!

CHAPTER THREE

The Baptism

*"We owed a debt we could never pay.
But Jesus Christ came paid the debt
He did not owe!"*

– Author Unknown

What Is Baptism?

A s stated earlier in this book, it seemed outsiders of the faith have a better or thorough knowledge of water baptism, the same baptism that many in the faith take casually. We therefore need to explore what it holds for us. This is

> "Colossians 2:14 -The Cross of Jesus was designed and intended as a means to an end, and an end to a means! Everything it's intended to end therefore ends in your life today! -2Cor. 6:2. And the door to and of His new life is yours forever [to walk through]!"
> -Saheed Ogunsola

what this book attempts to bring to light, not the academic definition or information, but the practical realities as seen in the works of salvation.

We don't just want to get dipped in water and come out soaked but with the fragrance of His knowledge that we may also walk in the newness of His life!

However, before delving into what baptism is, we may do well to first understand **the why of baptism**. In the first place, this is how baptism came to light in the Bible, especially in the New Testament. Though baptism had been even in the old times, it only came to full light in the New Testament so that God's full thought behind it, is practical reality in His Son, may be brought into full view for us.

Remember, God has in these last times chosen to speak unto us in and through His Son, and no one else! (Hebrews 1:1). So outside the Son, God isn't there! Period! And baptism, like every other thing, came to full light in and through Him! (2 Timothy 1:10).

30

"Who hath saved us, and called us with an holy calling, not according to our works, but according to his own purpose and grace, which was given us in Christ Jesus before the world began, But is now made manifest by the appearing of our Saviour Jesus Christ, who hath abolished death, and hath brought life and immortality to light through the gospel."
– 2 Timothy 1:19-10.

The reason for baptism was what we learned first through John the Baptizer's discourse with the Pharisees and those sent to query him, and thereafter we can understand better what baptism, and water baptism for that matter, truly is!

The Why of Baptism

"And I knew him not: but that he should be made manifest to Israel, therefore am I come baptizing with water... And I saw, and bare record that this is the Son of God." – John 1:33-34.

Through the ministry of John, we saw that **baptism was the key of bringing the Lamb of God to light, out of obscurity.** Manifestation or the unveiling of a hidden identity or the hidden man was the core reason for baptism. You see, God's ultimate provision of ending captivity was already provided, His Lamb of sacrifice was among the people but the people knew Him not. Therefore, that He might be made manifest, water baptism was commanded of the Lord, and John the Baptizer complied!

Water baptism was therefore brought forth for the purpose of **unveiling what is behind the scenes, in the work of redemption, and bringing forth to light that which God**

has wrought and is doing in His new creation. We may never truly know the full depth of the things of God in our redemption but this order He gave to John was to give us a glimpse.

This is very much like the case of the twelve spies who were sent to have a glimpse of the promised land before the whole nation was to make the practical and final entry into the same. Their testimony changed everything!

May the Lord therefore open your eyes, through the key of water baptism, to see all that has been fully wrought for you in redemption and begin to take practical steps into your inheritance!

Beloved, there is a treasure hidden in your life, and the light of life is the only means of bringing it out! (2Cor. 4:7). You never can know who you are or can be until you come to salvation! There are things only known to God, and salvation through Jesus Christ is the only way of separating the chaff from the wheat. His life is the light which reveals, uncovers and can help manifest those hidden things.

> *"In the affairs of man, death had been thought to be final until Jesus Christ came and showed that death is not final but His life."*
> *- Saheed Ogunsola*

"Who hath saved us, and called us with an holy calling... made manifest by the appearing of our Saviour Jesus Christ, who hath abolished death, and hath brought life and immortality to light through the gospel." – 2 Timothy 1:19-10.

In the affairs of man, death had been thought to be final until Jesus Christ came and showed that death is not final but His life. So, there is no way that which has been given before the world began can come to full light without the One who had been before time, and by Whom all things came to be!

The Saviour, Deliverer, whom the Jews desired, cried for and sought diligently after was already among them but they knew Him not (John 1:10-11). And the key to His manifestation among them was water baptism!

"And this is the record of John, when the Jews sent priests and Levites from Jerusalem to ask him, Who art thou? And he confessed, and denied not; but confessed, I am not the Christ.

And they asked him, What then? Art thou Elias? And he saith, I am not. Art thou that prophet? And he answered, No. Then said they unto him, Who art thou? that we may give an answer to them that sent us. What sayest thou of thyself?

He said, I am the voice of one crying in the wilderness, Make straight the way of the Lord, as said [by] the prophet Esaias. And they which were sent were of the Pharisees.

And they asked him, and said unto him, <u>Why baptizest thou then</u>, if thou be not that Christ, nor Elias, neither that prophet? John answered them, saying, I baptize with water: but there standeth one among you, whom ye know not; He it is, who coming after me is preferred before me, whose shoe's latchet I am not worthy to unloose.

...This is he of whom I said, After me cometh a man which is preferred before me: for he was before me. And I knew him not:

but that he should be made manifest to Israel, therefore am I come baptizing with water." – John 1:19-31.

The ridiculous was commanded that the miraculous may be manifest for all! This has always been the order of things with God who uses foolish things to confound the wise! He shall therefore make your life a wonder!

The world doesn't know Him, and thus ignorant about your potentials through Him. You are His hidden treasure in the world as His treasure is also hidden in your life (I John 3:1). The world shall therefore be shocked when your manifestation begins!

Even when the Holy Spirit came down at Pentecost, and the disciples were baptized in Him at the Upper Room, everyone was shocked at what they saw for Galileans were never accounted as amounting so much in the eyes of the elites of those days!

"And they were all amazed and marvelled, saying one to another, Behold, are not all these which speak Galilaeans?"
– Acts 2:87.

Jesus Himself confirmed that the laws and prophets prophesied until John, and since then, the Kingdom of God is preached, implying the manifestation began! John's ministry, using water baptism, was used as a door from the old to the new!

"The law and the prophets were until John: since that time the kingdom of God is preached, and every man presseth into it."
– Luke 16:16.

The personal understanding of water baptism therefore revolutionized my life and made me discover the man God is after, the man of God's making! As a token, water baptism's purpose therefore is to bring to light that which lies buried, hidden away from the eyes of the natural man.

The Definition of Baptism

The ritual or ceremony of cleansing is not exclusive to Judaism or Christianity. Many religions especially among the Orientals engage in one form of religious or spiritual cleansing or one form of washing or the other.

> *"Therefore we are buried with him by baptism unto death that like has Christ was raised up from the dead by the glory of the Father, even so we also should walk in the newness of life."*
> *-Romans 6:4*

Now, there are different types of baptisms and many ideas about baptism, as there are many teachers. Hebrews 6:2 which mentions the **doctrine of baptisms** goes to affirm that there are many types of baptisms.

However, in its simplest meaning or principle, **baptism is a symbolic spiritual exercise essentially for a change of state of an item to be immersed**, and in the case of water baptism in the name of the Lord Jesus Christ. It's about change of status, state or life. Some refer to this as the process of disambiguation.

Ambiguity refers to something doubtful, having many sides, not clean, clear or straightforward, and the process of removing what stands as impurity is the disambiguation. Baptism is **the immersion of an element with impurity into a cleaning agent for its uncleanness to be removed. The coming out of the baptized makes it a new or renewed material.**

Water baptism is a sacrament -sign, token or symbol of **an outward and visible sign of the inward and invisible action in where God works on the one being baptized for transformation.** This marks the beginning of a new relationship with God and the baptized person.

Now, it worth being noted that if water baptism represents what took place at salvation, then the New Testament believer should understand that he/she has a change of identity or citizenship at salvation. This is a vital key water baptism shows.

Now, water baptism process involves immersion into a body of water, signifying death and burial, thereby an end to a man's nature, status or citizenship, and in being raised out from the water, the coming out of an entirely new person with a new nature, status or citizenship.

Gentiles or non-Jews, who wish or desire to become Jews and enter Judaism, go through the process of circumcision and water baptism among other rituals for their conversion. These converts are called **Proselytes.** The Abrahamic circumcision enjoins them into covenant with God while **the water baptism signifies and confirms their change of citizenship.**

Now, there are Christian denominations today that do not believe nor practice the doctrine of baptism citing Matthew 3:11 where John the Baptizer says,

"I indeed baptize you with water unto repentance: but he that cometh after me is mightier than I, whose shoes I am not worthy to bear: he shall baptize you with the Holy Ghost, and with fire:" – Matthew 3:11.

> *"God sometimes takes us into troubled waters not to drown us but to cleans us and bring forth a new man."*
> -Author nknown

By this statement, according to their own view, water baptism was only something that happened until or that led to the time Jesus Christ came, but thenceforth, we have moved on to the inward baptisms that Christ does in every believer. By this reason, according to them, it is meaningless to conduct water baptism.

However, **water baptism is simply a symbolic act that, among other things, is a powerful reminder of the process and price of redemption Jesus Christ paid to save us.** The lowering into the water is symbolic of how the natural man who is dead in sins and trespasses is buried out of God's sight. By that act, the old life is ended! And the coming out of the water is symbolic of how, through our faith in Jesus Christ, we are saved and raised from death with Him having received His eternal life.

The earlier Christians believed so much in the symbolic power of baptism that even the dead were baptized so that they could resurrect with the Lord!

"Else what shall they do which are baptized for the dead, if the dead rise not at all? why are they then baptized for the dead?"
– I Cor. 15:29.

Water baptism therefore opens our eyes to our new status as kingdom citizens of heaven, God's very dear sons!

The Origin of Baptism

By the Holy Ghost and scriptures, Apostle Paul explained that the Old Testament Israel went through a type of baptism when they crossed the Red Sea and while under the cloud-cover with Moses.

"Moreover, brethren, I would not that ye should be ignorant, how that all our fathers were under the cloud, and all passed through the sea; And were all baptized unto Moses in the cloud and in the sea." – I Cor. 10:1-2.

Moses stood here as a type of deliverer. The children of Israel were baptized unto him in the Red sea and the cloud which are figures of the New Testament believer's baptism unto Jesus in His death and when He was lifted, and seated in the heavenlies! (Ephesians 2:1, 5-6)

Though Israel was delivered from the slavery in Egypt but they were not yet saved until they crossed the Red sea when they were baptized unto Moses. The Egyptians who assayed to do the same perished therein! **The Red sea was a place of the deep, a place of death for those not approved of God.**

Remember, when John baptized men, **heaven opened upon only one man – the only man recognized by heaven!**

Jesus Christ may have died and paid for the sin of the whole world but **no man is saved yet until such receives Jesus Christ into his or her life as Lord and Saviour, that is, gets baptized by the Holy Spirit into Him at salvation!**

Also throughout the first five books of the Old Testament, God educated Israel, through the law and priesthood, on the difference between clean and unclean people, animals and objects. And we see that water was majorly used as a purifying agent.

The book of Leviticus is rooted and full of information on all manner of cleansings for men and objects with different purifying agents as commanded by God.

In fulfilling priestly duties, the Levites were commanded to bathe themselves completely before they entered the tabernacle, and in addition, to emphasize cleanliness further, a great water basin (Laver) was constructed and erected for that purpose. This is where the idea of water ablution – a type of water baptism or cleansing originated from.

Also, God commanded through Moses that a stranger or Gentile who wanted to join himself to Israel was to be subject to the same law: *"One law shall be for the native-born and for the stranger who dwells among you"* (Exodus 12:49). The ordained law pertained not only to circumcision and the dietary laws but also to the washings (Leviticus 17:15).

The root word from which we get the words baptize, baptism and baptized carries the meaning of being covered wholly with a fluid or cleansing agent. Recognizing this meaning, the Jewish New Testament identifies John the Baptist as "the Immerser" or the Baptizer as he immersed in water those who came to him.

The Opened Heaven

"And Jesus, when he was baptized, went up straightway out of the water: and, lo, the heavens were opened unto him, and he saw the Spirit of God descending like a dove, and lighting upon him: And lo a voice from heaven, saying, This is my beloved Son, in whom I am well pleased." – Matthew 3:16-12.

"And I knew him not: but that he should be made manifest to Israel, therefore am I come baptizing with water. And John bare record, saying, I saw the Spirit descending from heaven like a dove, and it abode upon him. And I knew him not: but he that sent me to baptize with water, the same said unto me, Upon whom thou shalt see the Spirit descending, and remaining on him, the same is he which baptizeth with the Holy Ghost. And I saw, and bare record that this is the Son of God." – John 1:33-34.

Multitudes were baptized by John but he saw heaven opened upon God's chosen One, and thereby testified in agreement with God about Jesus' identity as the Son of God.

As earlier stated, baptism or ceremonial washings are not peculiar to Judaism or Christianity. Check out many religions even in the present age as they do all manner of washings or ablutions that seem to point to holiness or godliness.

But remember, as with the multitudes, **heaven opened only upon the man God has chosen for Himself!** And God has testified about His Son before the whole world. Who can dispute this?

Therefore, no matter the depth of purity being promoted by any religion, if it's outside the person of the Lord Jesus Christ, it's under closed heaven! It's a closed case with heaven! There is no eternal value in it! Period!

So, water baptism is beyond church ritual, **God used it to publicly announce, unveil and attest to His Son, the Man in whom His Spirit has found rest.** Therefore, because of Jesus Christ, Christianity stands alone in its class with God.

By the same token, open heavens shall be your portion! The secret place of the Most High shall stand you out among others! As in Egypt, when God put distinction between Egyptians and Israel (Exodus 11:7), exemption from calamity through the blood of His cross shall be your lot!

So when you are IN Christ, you should expect to live your new life under opened heavens! It's an experience every believer must look forward to! There should be no doubt in your mind as to this great work of redemption already wrought for you!

Agents and Elements of Cleansing

"John answered, saying unto them all, I indeed baptize you with water; but one mightier than I cometh, the latchet of whose shoes

41

I am not worthy to unloose: he shall baptize you with the Holy Ghost and with fire."- Luke 3:16.

Throughout scriptures, beginning with the Old Testament, there are basically three elements God ordained or instructed to be used as cleansing agents for the removal of impurities. **Prophetically, these elements in a way foretell what the Messiah will eventually utilize in the birthing of the coming age.**

The elements of cleansing or sanctification which are **water, blood and fire,** are therefore more manifest in the ministry or operation of the Levites and Priests.

*"And Eleazar the priest said unto the men of war which went to the battle, This is the ordinance of the law which the LORD commanded Moses; Only the gold, and the silver, the brass, the iron, the tin, and the lead, Every thing that may abide the fire, ye shall make it go through the fire, and it shall be clean: nevertheless it shall be purified with the water of separation: and all that abideth not the fire ye shall make go through the water. And ye shall wash your clothes on the seventh day, and ye shall be clean, and afterward ye shall come into the camp."
– Numbers 31:21-24.*

From the statements of John the Baptizer, these three elements are manifest – **water, the Holy Spirit, and fire,** with the blood being silent and substituted now with the Holy Ghost, as **blood signifies life, new life!**

For blood to be used in cleansing by the priests an animal has to be used. For the blood to be obtained the animal has to be slaughtered. The slaying of that animal is the end of its life in the flesh so that its hidden life in the blood can be released and used.

In the books of Hebrews 12:24, and I Peter 1:2, we have the word **"sprinkling" of the blood by Jesus Christ upon every believer.** That word "Sprinkling" is a type of the symbolic cleansing by the Old Testament priests.

So, even in the New Testament, our **cleansing by the blood** is still there which precedes the coming of the Holy Spirit. The baptism with these elements will not only remove impurities but turn the baptized into what God can use, just as the priests or Levites could not enter into their offices or official positions in the things pertaining to God until the cleansing rituals have been carried out.

As in the Old Testament cleansing and washings, we find the same washing agents in the New Testament employed by God in and through Jesus Christ for our salvation. You can never be of any effective Kingdom use with God until your life comes under the operation of these cleansing agents.

Let's see them in the New Testament:

"That he might sanctify and cleanse it with the washing of water by the word, That he might present it to himself a glorious church, not having spot, or wrinkle, or any such thing; but that it should be holy and without blemish." – Ephesians 5:26-27

"But after that the kindness and love of God our Saviour toward man appeared, Not by works of righteousness which we have done, but according to his mercy he saved us, by the washing of regeneration, and renewing of the Holy Ghost; Which he shed

on us abundantly through Jesus Christ our Saviour."
– Tutus 3:4-6.

"And to Jesus the mediator of the new covenant, and to the blood of sprinkling, that speaketh better things than that of Abel."
- Hebrews 12:24 .

"Elect according to the foreknowledge of God the Father, through sanctification of the Spirit, unto obedience and sprinkling of the blood of Jesus Christ: Grace unto you, and peace, be multiplied." – I Peter 1:2 .

Now, if baptism is part of the process of changing from one state to a new or renewed state, from one humanity or citizenship unto another, and Jesus came preaching the Gospel of the Kingdom to which He was inviting all men, then His baptism has been employed to signify the change from one humanity to another, from the being citizen of the world into heavenly Kingdom citizen.

Therefore, it is said that **those who believed and received Jesus Christ as their Lord and Saviour may be in the world, but are not of the world.** They have been redeemed out from the world unto God. They are now ambassadors of another kingdom in the world!

Now, the prince of this age, Satan, has no claim over such people any longer! They are not his own, he has no claim nor right over them.

"For our conversation [community, citizenship] is in heaven; from whence also we look for the Saviour, the Lord Jesus Christ:"
– Philippians 3:20 (KJV) (Emphasis added)

44

"For our country is in heaven; from where the Saviour for whom we are waiting will come, even the Lord Jesus Christ:"
– Philippians 3:20 (BBE-Bible in Basic English).

"We, however, are citizens of heaven, and we eagerly wait for our Savior, the Lord Jesus Christ, to come from heaven."
– Philippians 3:20 (GNB -Good News Bible).

Know therefore who and whose you are if you are born again. You must understand your root, and the new nature imputed into you, so that you don't live as outsiders of Christ's Kingdom. You are a pilgrim and stranger in this world but a citizen of heaven! Your mind must be renewed and imbued with this new status.

The declaration of Jesus Christ as Son of God, after coming out from the water during baptism by John was a pointer to or foretelling of His declaration as the Son of God after resurrection from death by the power of the Holy Spirit. So, **the man who came out from the water is the resurrected man, a new man of the citizen of heaven!**

"John answered them, saying, <u>I baptize with water:</u> but there standeth one among you, whom ye know not; And I knew him not: but he that sent me to baptize with water, the same said unto me, Upon whom thou shalt see the Spirit descending, and remaining on him, the same is he which baptizeth with the Holy Ghost. And I saw, and bare record that this is the Son of God."
- John 1:26, 33-34.

"Paul, a servant of Jesus Christ, called to be an apostle, separated unto the gospel of God, (Which he had promised afore by his prophets in the holy scriptures,) Concerning his Son Jesus Christ

our Lord, which was made of the seed of David according to the flesh, And declared to be the Son of God with power, according to the spirit of holiness, by the resurrection from the dead."
– Romans 1:1-4:

Glory to God, we have been made alive and raised together with Him! (Ephesians 2:1, 5-6).

In conclusion, whether baptism is by water, blood, fire or the Holy Ghost, the principal intention is a new vessel, after God's order, fit ultimately for God's use. **Baptism is the door and gateway of exit for the old and the entry of the new creation of God!**

The Understanding of the Pharisees

"For I say unto you, Among those that are born of women there is not a greater prophet than John the Baptist: but he that is least in the kingdom of God is greater than he. And all the people that heard him, and the publicans, justified God, being baptized with the baptism of John.

But the Pharisees and lawyers rejected the counsel of God against themselves, being not baptized of him."
– Luke 7:28-30.

We know in part, and therefore, prophesy in part, but may what you know, or think you know, never become the stumbling block to what you should know of the Lord! This was the case of the teachers of the law or lawyers, the Sadducees and the Pharisees. The idea of all types of baptism was not new to the Pharisees, scribes and teachers of the law but what John the Baptizer began to do puzzled them. It

46

seemed ridiculous since, according to them, they have always followed the tradition of the fathers handed down to them, the bulk of which is the diverse ceremonies of cleansing. As doers of the tradition of the elders, they considered themselves a clean breed of men and not impure nor sinners.

> *"The most blessed results are not always in the realm where there is a great comprehending of truth, but more often in the realm where there is a simplicity, honesty, and openness of spirit. Some people are far too well informed to LIVE..."*
> - T. Austin-Sparks

However, they were wrong on the plans of God for instructing John's baptism. Their pride in what they received from their fathers became a stumbling block that kept them out of the plans of God!

Taking of baths and washing of feet after public outings, washing of hands before eating and some other ceremonial ablutions were all regarded as a one form of baptism or the other. These are normal things with them but could not figure how they could publicly come and subject themselves from their exalted positions to baptism in a river, in a common place with common people! They were puffed up in their knowledge.

"Then came together unto him the Pharisees, and certain of the scribes, which came from Jerusalem. And when they saw some of his disciples eat bread with defiled, that is to say, with unwashen, hands, they found fault.

For the Pharisees, and all the Jews, <u>except</u> they wash their hands oft, eat not, holding the tradition of the elders. And when they come from the market, except they wash, they eat not. And many other things there be, which they have received to hold, as the washing of cups, and pots, brasen vessels, and of tables."
– Mark 7:1-4.

From this scripture, it is very clear about the everyday acts of the Pharisees when it comes to cleanliness. All manner of washings or ablutions were common to them which they strictly followed. It was therefore a "ridiculous" thing for John to ask them to come and baptize in water openly when they were not sinners but "clean" people.

"Then the Pharisees and scribes asked him, Why walk not thy disciples according to the tradition of the elders, but eat bread with unwashen hands?

He answered and said unto them, Well hath Esaias prophesied of you hypocrites, as it is written, This people honoureth me with their lips, but their heart is far from me. Howbeit in vain do they worship me, teaching for doctrines the commandments of men. For laying aside the commandment of God, ye hold the tradition of men, as the washing of pots and cups: and many other such like things ye do.

And he said unto them, Full well ye reject the commandment of God, that ye may keep your own tradition."- Mark 7:5-9.

Since John's baptism was for remission of sins, and the leaders never considered themselves sinners, they rejected his ministry and assignment.

48

"John did baptize in the wilderness, and preach the baptism of repentance for the remission of sins." – Mark 1:4.

The Gentiles and other class of men who do not follow the law, especially those things received by tradition from the elders, were those the Pharisees considered as sinners who needed John's baptism.

Remember, everyone went unto John confessing their sins.

"And there went out unto him all the land of Judaea, and they of Jerusalem, and were all baptized of him in the river of Jordan, confessing their sins." – Mark 1:5.

The idea is that those confessing their sins were renouncing who they were, as they were being immersed in the water, and therefore received a new identity as they were raised out from the water. They came out as new men whose sins have been forgiven!

Now the Pharisees see themselves already as Jews, so why would they need to go through a process meant for sinners or non-Jews? They considered themselves God's chosen sons of Abraham, why would they need to go through the process meant for those who were not naturally the children of Abraham through Isaac?

John's baptism was baffling and humiliating for them. They therefore rejected being baptized by him. However, in rejecting John the Baptizer's ministry, they rejected God's counsel for themselves as John had clearly stated that he was instructed of the Lord to baptize. Therefore his actions were not his idea but express instructions from above.

And Jesus Christ soon opened up their error and hypocrisy.

"And they come again to Jerusalem: and as he was walking in the temple, there come to him the chief priests, and the scribes, and the elders, And say unto him, By what authority doest thou these things? and who gave thee this authority to do these things?

And Jesus answered and said unto them, I will also ask of you one question, and answer me, and I will tell you by what authority I do these things.

The baptism of John, was it from heaven, or of men? answer me.

And they reasoned with themselves, saying, If we shall say, From heaven; he will say, Why then did ye not believe him? But if we shall say, Of men; they feared the people: for all men counted John, that he was a prophet indeed.

And they answered and said unto Jesus, We cannot tell. And Jesus answering saith unto them, Neither do I tell you by what authority I do these things." – Mark 11:27-33.

Your mockers are also going into perpetual silence!

God is in the process of a new creation, a new world is in view. All that must be part of it must go through the process of His baptism unto His Son. And the water baptism is simply the foreshadow of the process of conversion from one humanity into another through His Son and the Holy Spirit.

Remember that the Lord Jesus also mentioned His own suffering as baptism. The process of His sufferings that will lead to the salvation of men was referred to by Him as baptism wherein all judgement and penalty of sins, transgressions and iniquities shall be placed on Him.

"But I have a baptism to be baptized with; and how am I straitened till it be accomplished!" – Luke 12:50.

"And Jesus going up to Jerusalem took the twelve disciples apart in the way, and said unto them, Behold, we go up to Jerusalem; and the Son of man shall be betrayed unto the chief priests and unto the scribes, and they shall condemn him to death, And shall deliver him to the Gentiles to mock, and to scourge, and to crucify him: and the third day he shall rise again.

Then came to him the mother of Zebedee's children with her sons, worshipping him, and desiring a certain thing of him. And he said unto her, What wilt thou? She saith unto him, Grant that these my two sons may sit, the one on thy right hand, and the other on the left, in thy kingdom.

But Jesus answered and said, Ye know not what ye ask. Are ye able to drink of the cup that I shall drink of, and to be baptized with the baptism that I am baptized with? They say unto him, We are able.

And he saith unto them, Ye shall drink indeed of my cup, and be baptized with the baptism that I am baptized with: but to sit on my right hand, and on my left, is not mine to give, but it shall be given to them for whom it is prepared of my Father. And when the ten heard it, they were moved with indignation against the two brethren." – Matthew 20:17-24.

51

Our water baptism is our identification with Him as He identified with us in the work of redemption. And as our substitute, He took upon Himself all our sin and punishments, and therefore with our faith in Him we are justified without works!

Fulfilling All Righteousness

"Then cometh Jesus from Galilee to Jordan unto John, to be baptized of him. But John forbad him, saying, I have need to be baptized of thee, and comest thou to me? And Jesus answering said unto him, Suffer it to be so now: for thus it becometh us to fulfil all righteousness. Then he suffered him."
– Matthew 3:13-15.

Jesus, the sinless man, had reasons for going for water baptism that even John didn't have an idea about. John was quite right in hesitating and requesting that he was the one who needed to be baptized of Him because all men are the ones who needed baptism from the Lord Jesus!

What sin was the sinless One going to confess? He is already the Man of heaven, which change of status is He still seeking? He is from God, God's Son, which transformation is the perfect One yet seeking? Many things as such must have been going through the mind of John.

So, why did Jesus go for John's baptism? For in their dialogue, Jesus said, *"it becometh us to fulfill all righteousness"*.

What could He mean by this?

To **"fulfill"** implies to carry out, to bring to realization, as a prophecy or promises. This means there is something in view which has to be realized or completed through obedience or steps to follow!

There is a form of rightness with God that has to be done – there is a way God had planned or ordained things and this has to be done. Among many things, we can deduce three vital keys or things with respect to His statement.

Firstly, how is righteousness obtained? It's simply through faith and obedience. Jesus came, humbled and submitted Himself to what the Father had instructed Him.

"Therefore doth my Father love me, because I lay down my life, that I might take it again. No man taketh it from me, but I lay it down of myself. I have power to lay it down, and I have power to take it again. This commandment have I received of my Father." – John 10:17-18.

Remember, baptism is simply a sacrament or symbol of deeper things. The Father had instructed the Son to lay down His life that He might pick it up again. Jesus therefore, in His faith, obedience and love for the Father's desire and will, willingly laid down His life!

"...Made himself of no reputation, and took upon him the form of a servant, and was made in the likeness of men: And being found in fashion as a man, he humbled himself, and became obedient unto death, even the death of the cross." – Philippians 2:7-8.

In His substitutionary death, the old man, old creature was crucified and buried out of sight. The sins of that man, which God had promised He will remember no more, was not only atoned for but buried in the sea of forgetfulness!

"This is the covenant that I will make with them after those days, saith the Lord, I will put my laws into their hearts, and in their minds will I write them; And their sins and iniquities will I remember no more. Now where remission of these is, there is no more offering for sin." – Hebrews 10:16-18.

Now, what has been taken out of God's sight doesn't exist again! What He's forgiven you, no one has the right to bring up again against you! Whatever He doesn't remember, no devil has any right to bring up, remind you and use against you!

Secondly, the prophets, law and Psalms had prophesied of the sufferings of Christ and the glory that would follow (I Peter 1:10). Jesus was thus stepping out in obedience for the fulfilment of that which had been written!

Thirdly, and most importantly, the Son must take His place as the first, forerunner and the lead in God's new creation! A new world, heaven and earth, is in view where righteousness dwells, and as in the old creation where everything came through the instrument of the Son, as the Lamb slain from the foundation of the world, **He had come again for that which is in view.**

More of this is dealt with in the later chapter of this book.

There are scriptures and prophecies that have to be fulfilled, with conditions, processes, people and places involved.

The Lord was therefore talking to John the Baptizer about taking out of God's sight (like the scapegoat), the old man

54

through burial, signified by the immersion in water, so that that which God is after, the new man, through the atoning sacrifice can be birthed.

> *"For he hath made him to be sin for us, who knew no sin; that we might be made the righteousness of God in him."*
> *-2Corithians 5:21*

Jordan was both a grave for burial of the old man, and a womb for the birth of the new man! The statement of Jesus to John was more than a religious statement, eternal counsels are involved.

However, let's still touch one more thing here.

The Scapegoat and Confession

In the Old Testament, during the process of sacrifices on the Day of Atonement, one of the goats used is referred to as the scapegoat, and this plays a significant role in our discourse.

What the high priest would do was to lay both hands on this goat and confess all the sins, iniquities and transgressions of the children of Israel upon this goat and thereafter release it into the wilderness, a land uninhabited. The scapegoat would thus bear all their sins and iniquities out of sight!

"And Aaron shall cast lots upon the two goats; one lot for the LORD, and the other lot for the scapegoat. And Aaron shall bring the goat upon which the LORD'S lot fell, and offer him for a sin offering. But the goat, on which the lot fell to be the scapegoat, shall be presented alive before the LORD, to make an atonement with him, and to let him go for a scapegoat into the wilderness.

And Aaron shall lay both his hands upon the head of the live goat, and confess over him all the iniquities of the children of Israel, and all their transgressions in all their sins, putting them upon the head of the goat, and shall send him away by the hand of a fit man into the wilderness: And the goat shall bear upon him all their iniquities unto a land not inhabited: and he shall let go the goat in the wilderness." – Leviticus 16:8-10, 21-22.

Now, you will do well to remember that Jesus, as the Lamb of God, came to take away the sin of the world (John 1:29).

One of the things that may have puzzled John, when Jesus came for baptism, was the fact that: here's a sinless man coming for baptism! Which sin was He going to confess? What wrong has He ever done that He would require forgiveness?

But remember, in His atoning work, God was going to lay upon Him the iniquity of us all (Isaiah 53:6). **And in bearing the iniquities, confession would be involved just as in the case of the scapegoat by the high priest.**

"All we like sheep have gone astray; we have turned every one to his own way; and the LORD hath laid on him the iniquity of us all. He shall see of the travail of his soul, and shall be satisfied: by his knowledge shall my righteous servant justify many; for he shall bear their iniquities." – Isaiah 53:6, 11.

Now, water baptism stands as the summary act of a great and mysterious work of redemption. **As others were confessing their sins when being baptized, what do we see Jesus doing when He too was being baptized?**

Scriptures rightly informs us **He was praying!** But then, what could He be praying?

We may not know precisely what Jesus was praying or saying, but with this symbolic act that points to His atoning work, **He was identifying with our sin - the sin of the whole world!** This place represents where He was taking our sin unto Himself, taking our place, being made sin, as the iniquity of us all was being laid upon Him!

One of the meanings of the word **"borne"**, written in Isaiah 53:4, implies to "accept, carry away". Therefore, He praying was His identifying with our sins, iniquities and transgressions.

Remember the scapegoat upon which the high priest would lay his hands, confessing the sins of the whole nation! (Leviticus 16:8, 20-22). And where did Jesus go after His baptism in Jordan? He went straight into the wilderness just like the scapegoat!

This identification with us is very crucial **because in our receiving His salvation, we also come in through confession.** Now, what is our own confession? We confess His Lordship and salvation of our souls.

As He identified with our sin or sins, we identify and receive the resultant work of His sacrifice – His righteousness! **You are not born again because you confessed all your sins,** all of which you can't even remember but **because you believe, receive and confess Jesus Christ as your Lord and Saviour.**

"But what saith it? The word is nigh thee, even in thy mouth, and in thy heart: that is, the word of faith, which we preach; That if thou shalt confess with thy mouth the Lord Jesus, and shalt believe in thine heart that God hath raised him from the dead, thou shalt be saved. For with the heart man believeth unto righteousness; and with the mouth confession is made unto salvation." – Romans 8:8-10.

In His great atoning work, as our sin offering and scapegoat, He took upon and unto Himself all our sin and iniquities. He took them out of sight where they shall never be seen again!

Then remember again, after the baptism of Jesus Christ, where did He go next? Yes, the wilderness! Just as the scapegoat of Old was released into the wilderness!

"And Jesus being full of the Holy Ghost returned from Jordan, and was led by the Spirit into the wilderness... And when the devil had ended all the temptation, he departed from him for a season. And Jesus returned in the power of the Spirit into Galilee: and there went out a fame of him through all the region round about." – Luke 4:1, 13-14.

Though the devil came and tempted Him, prying for access into His life, at the end he had to leave Him because he had nothing in Him, and Jesus returned in the power of the Holy Spirit and began to overthrow all the works of the devil.

By the power of His redemption blood, whatever remains as the work of the devil in and over your life, they shall be ended today!

The Nicodemus Dialogue

The case of baptism was brought up by Jesus while in dialogue with Nicodemus essentially because he was a Pharisee and member of the Sanhedrin. As earlier stated, this crop of very learned people had rejected the baptism of John.

"There was a man of the Pharisees, named Nicodemus, a ruler of the Jews: The same came to Jesus by night, and said unto him, Rabbi, we know that thou art a teacher come from God: for no man can do these miracles that thou doest, except God be with him.

Jesus answered and said unto him, Verily, verily, I say unto thee, Except a man be born again, he cannot see the kingdom of God. Nicodemus saith unto him, How can a man be born when he is old? can he enter the second time into his mother's womb, and be born?

Jesus answered, Verily, verily, I say unto thee, Except a man be born of water and of the Spirit, he cannot enter into the kingdom of God. That which is born of the flesh is flesh; and that which is born of the Spirit is spirit. Marvel not that I said unto thee, Ye must be born again." – John 3:1-7

> "Miracles are a retelling in small letters of the very same story which is written across the whole world for some of us to see."- CS Lewis

Nicodemus came to get answer to what had kept nudging his heart since Jesus showed up and was confessed by John the baptizer to be the long awaited One, with signs following His ministry. Nicodemus confessed what had also registered in the hearts of the Pharisees but not publicly acknowledged that the Lord Jesus was the God sent teacher and that His works were not ordinary but God wrought.

Nicodemus came talking about the visible works but Christ was quick to point him to where their error lay, the starting and important point where the Pharisees had got it all wrong in the sense of rejecting the counsel of God. And that for them to come into God's new scheme of things, being born of the water and of the Holy Spirit is non-negotiable!

The Lord was invariably sending him back to square one!

You see, in refusing to be baptized by John the Baptizer, the Pharisees completely rejected God's counsel and thus kept themselves outside the kingdom of God, and those who believed John were going ahead of them!

"And all the people that heard him, and the publicans, justified God, being baptized with the baptism of John. But the Pharisees and lawyers rejected the counsel of God against themselves, being not baptized of him." – Luke 7:29-30.

"...Verily I say unto you, That the publicans and the harlots go into the kingdom of God before you. For John came unto you in the way of righteousness, and ye believed him not: but the publicans and the harlots believed him: and ye, when ye had seen it, repented not afterward, that ye might believe him." – Matthew 21:32-32.

"...Except a man be born of water and of the Spirit, he cannot enter into the kingdom of God." – John 3:5.

Whatever the Pharisees thought they knew became a stumbling block regarding what more they should have come to know of God and enjoy in His work! They were not humble enough to enter into God's new move, and therefore kept themselves out.

Now, does it mean if you don't get baptized in water that your salvation is incomplete? No! But if you have the opportunity of going through it, don't hesitate. The statement in John 3:5 was essentially because the Pharisees had rejected the counsel of God by not believing and submitting to John's baptism.

When we become born again, we are already baptised into the body of Jesus Christ through the ministry of the Holy Spirit. Water baptism is the act which represents what has already taken place in the spirit and an open confession to the world about our new citizenship.

"He that believeth and is baptized shall be saved; but he that believeth not shall be damned."- Mark 16:16.

Jesus said those who shall be damned are those *"that believeth not..."*. So baptism is not what gets you saved but faith in Him – the Saviour. However, if you have opportunity to do water baptism, never hesitate! It is an act of faith – the "evidence" of things not seen! (Hebrews 11:1).

Therefore in rejecting John's testimony and counsel, the Pharisees rejected Jesus Christ the Lamb of God, and the means of provision for their salvation. They inevitably set themselves in opposition against God whom they claim to represent. And guess who plotted the death and crucifixion of Jesus? Yes, those same rulers!

61

Water baptism is the bold, public declaration by every believer of the passing away of the old life and manifestation of the new life that is in Christ Jesus - "confession" of change of citizenship from one humanity to another.

There is a world of living knowledge and testimony when we humble ourselves to follow God's instructions. Whatever God says, He has eternal bliss in view, and no one misses out in obeying Him. Self-righteousness ruined the leaders of Israel.

May you never miss out in the great treasures that salvation holds for you!

CHAPTER FOUR

The Man of New Beginning!

*"Jesus Christ did not come into
this world to make bad people good;
He came into this world to make
dead people live."*

- Lee Strobel

63

The Secret Things

> *"The secret things belong unto the LORD our God: but those things which are revealed belong unto us and to our children for ever, that we may do all the words of this law."*
> – Deut. 29:29.

> *"...And that he would shew thee the secrets of wisdom, that they are double to that which is!"-Job 11:6.*

The incarnation of God's word, and the subsequent manifestation in and through Jesus Christ is part of His last days revelation of things hidden from the foundation of the world. Foundations are not usually visible to the eye, but God would have us know His works, appreciate them and appreciate in them! The appearance and presence of our Lord Jesus Christ is to bring to light and manifestation the full purpose of God.

Scripture says, by His appearance He cancelled out death, and then brought life and immortality to light!

> *"Who hath saved us, and called us with an holy calling, not according to our works, but according to his own purpose and grace, which was given us in Christ Jesus before the world began, But is now made manifest by the appearing of our Saviour Jesus Christ, who hath abolished death, and hath brought life and immortality to light through the gospel."*
> - 2 Timothy 1:9-10.

Every word Jesus shared, every act He performed, and every step He took were all geared toward the unfolding of the things hidden for the benefits of those who believe and receive Him!

64

"All these things spake Jesus unto the multitude in parables; and without a parable spake he not unto them: That it might be fulfilled which was spoken by the prophet, saying, I will open my mouth in parables; I will utter things which have been kept secret from the foundation of the world." -Matthew 13:34-35.

These secrets are the things that give the believer an edge in the race of life. Christ came to bring hidden knowledge to light that the recipients of the same might shine as stars among others. The lack of this knowledge seems to be the chief reason behind the arrests in many lives.

"...But they regard not the work of the LORD, neither consider the operation of his hands. Therefore my people are gone into captivity, because they have no knowledge: and their honourable men are famished, and their multitude dried up with thirst."-Isaiah 5:12-13.

Knowledge opens the door to liberty. Knowledge is light, it opens up what was once covered by darkness and makes ways for progress. When we pursue the knowledge of our Saviour, then the knowledge of things will be easier to secure.

The Lifted Serpent

"Moreover the word of the LORD came unto me, saying, Son of man, take up a lamentation upon the king of Tyrus, and say unto him, Thus saith the Lord GOD; <u>Thou sealest up the sum, full of wisdom, and perfect in beauty.</u>

Thou hast been in Eden the garden of God; every precious stone was thy covering, the sardius, topaz, and the diamond, the beryl, the onyx, and the jasper, the sapphire, the emerald, and the carbuncle, and gold: the workmanship of thy tabrets and of thy pipes was prepared in thee in the day that thou wast created. Thou art the anointed cherub that covereth; and I have set thee so: thou wast upon the holy mountain of God; thou hast walked up and down in the midst of the stones of fire.

Thou wast perfect in thy ways from the day that thou wast created, till iniquity was found in thee." - Ezekiel 28:11-15.

Bible scholars have made us understand that this scripture was addressing Lucifer, the power behind the man being seemingly addressed – the king of Tyrus. This was like the case when Jesus was addressing Satan while looking at Peter (Matthew. 16:23), and also when He was speaking to Satan after giving the sop to Judas Iscariot (John 13:37).

From this quoted scripture, we see Lucifer the illuminating angel became corrupted and ended up as Satan – the adversary of anything and everything that has to do with Jehovah God.

We are told in this scripture that the one who represent the evil one was full of wisdom. It's virtually as saying the enemy behind him was full of wisdom. Quite right, the enemy has shown much subtlety. **However, being given wisdom is not the same as being the fountain of wisdom itself!**

Satan may be full of "wisdom" but Jesus Christ Himself is the wisdom of God. He is the embodiment of God's wisdom in every way!

And our God knows how to take the battle to the enemy's very territory and beat him at his game! Then you'll find that,

66

out of the eater comes the meat and out of the strong comes sweetness!

As the scripture says, *"the deceived and the deceiver are his!"* (Job 12:16); so the Lord in His own unparalleled, unlearned wisdom made foolish the wisdom of the world, and the powers behind the world!

Through subtlety, the adversary conned the first man and his wife into sin. God using His own irrefutable wisdom, He destroyed the wisdom of those who say they are wise! And He is still using the foolishness of the Cross to overthrow the wisdom outside His own!

"With him is strength and wisdom: the deceived and the deceiver are his. He leadeth counsellors away spoiled, and maketh the judges fools."- Job 12:16-17.

As part of the hidden works in Jordan, Jesus Christ our Lord revealed that as the serpent was lifted up in the wilderness, so He was going to be lifted that whosoever looked at Him, believed in Him shall be saved from the poison and death through the serpent's bite. This implies His wisdom is able to annul and overturn every satanic wisdom set against your life! (IJohn 3:8)

Though, we do not intend, in this book, to go into the full discourse of what happened in Numbers 21:4-9, however, we need to point out that the events here form part of what Christ came to accomplish for us in the redemption works. We see that murmuring against God brought judgment using the serpent.

The lifting of the Son of Man, Jesus Christ, on the wooden cross as foreshadowed in the fiery serpent that Moses hung on a pole is also part of what happened that the waters of Jordan represent. It's all part of the hidden works now revealed in Him.

The Son of Man – His Lifting

"And I, if I be lifted up from the earth, will draw all men unto me."- John 12:32.

John 12:32 is one of those misunderstood, misquoted and misapplied scriptures. Most people have used this scripture to depict lifting up the name of Jesus Christ in praise. And by this, we will see that the scripture has often been taken out of its context.

Though scriptures point to the fact that the Messiah will be exalted, lifted and shall be very high (Isaiah 52:13) which ultimately would cause believers to be raised up with Him to the heavenly places, however in this context the Lord wasn't talking about Himself being lifted in praise, He was indicating the manner of death He would die and bring redemption to man.

When we understand what happened here, then what happened in Jordan, and brought about our new creation, will be clearer than ever for us to enjoy the riches of redemption.

The Lord was talking about judgement and the prince of this world being overthrown when He mentioned His own lifting up in this scripture.

The word **"men"** was not in the original text and so should not be read with the scripture.

"Now is the judgment of this world: now shall the prince of this world be cast out. <u>And I, if I</u> be lifted up from the earth, will draw all men unto me. " – John 12:31-32.

Also, there are quite some people who have had struggles with this same scripture in another way.

The word translated **"judgement"** here is the English word for **"crisis"**. And by this crisis the prince of this world or cosmos –physical world shall be cast out.

While many say that the Lord was referring to the devil in this scripture (John 12:31), there are Bible Scholars who said that Jesus was actually referring to Himself as **"the Prince of this world"** because of two things.

The reasons for their argument are: firstly, the word translated **"world"** is the word for **"cosmos"** – the physical arrangement of creation or physical world; and secondly, because of Christ's suffering and eventual death for the salvation of mankind.

And by His death He was *"cast out"* of the earth or the created world.

However, believers should note that the crisis, punishment or agonies Jesus was put through ended up as a grave error for Satan and all the forces of darkness (ICor. 2:8). By His death, Jesus fulfilled the law, paid for sin, condemned sin in His flesh, dethroned Satan as the god of this world as He, Jesus Christ, received all authority in heaven and on earth, and obtained the keys of hell and death!

"I am he that liveth, and was dead; and, behold, I am alive for evermore, Amen; and have the keys of hell and of death."
– Revelation 1:18.

Now, at the end of the day, who was *"cast out"* of God's creation? The devil of course! The powers of darkness lost dominion over that which is the Lord's own, forever!

Scriptures tell us that the law has dominion over a man as long as he lives (Romans 7:1). Therefore in His death the dominion of Satan through man's sin when he violated God's law was ended.

"But now we are delivered from the law that being dead wherein we were held..."-Romans 7:6.

Moreso, in Matthew 4:8-9, during the temptation of Jesus in the wilderness, didn't the devil inform Him that the kingdoms of this world was in his hands and that he was ready to give it whosoever he would? Did Jesus dispute the devil's control over the kingdoms of this world at that time? No!

Also, remember that scripture says:

"And the great dragon was cast out, that old serpent, called the Devil, and Satan, which deceiveth the whole world: he was cast out into the earth, and his angels were cast out with him. And I heard a loud voice saying in heaven, Now is come salvation,

and strength, and the kingdom of our God, and the power of his Christ: for the accuser of our brethren is cast down, which accused them before our God day and night."
– Revelation 12:8-9.

Who was now cast out? Who lost place and position of control? Definitely not Jesus but the adversary, the devil! Jesus Christ is Lord forever!

What many scholars overlooked was the fact that in the same statement Jesus said, *"...And I, IF I be lifted up from the earth, I will draw all unto Me."* What was Jesus going to draw unto Himself? Of course, **all judgment or crisis!**

The Lord Jesus, as the Lamb of God, being made sin for us drew all judgement, crisis, suffering, punishment unto Himself! All sin and the wrath of God regarding sin was laid on Him because He was made sin for us, even though He knew no sin, so that we might be made the righteousness of God! The crisis is the chastisement for our sin which was laid on Him (Isaiah 53:5).

On the Cross, all the judgement of sin was laid upon Him! He drew all unto Himself, not leaving anything behind! Remember, before He committed His Spirit unto the Father, Jesus said, *"Father forgive them..."* as He drew all sin and the sin of their ignorance unto Himself (Luke 23:34). Then, it was finished!

"Then said Jesus, Father, forgive them; for they know not what they do..."- Luke 23:34.

The penalty, punishment for sin, and its power was ended by His perfect sacrifice as the scripture says, there remaineth no more sacrifice for sin (Hebrews 10:12, 14, 18). It is all now perfected in Christ!

Now, the prince of the darkness of this world no longer has any legal right over those who look to Jesus Christ – believed and received Him by faith, for their sins are no more. The ground for accusation is no more! Therefore, **there exist no more legal ground for the devil and his agents to lord it over you, again!**

Under the New Covenant, God promised that their sins and iniquities He will remember no more! What you remember no more has left you, and things are back to the original. **His perfect work on the cross was so perfect that it was as if you never sinned before!** Nothing ever can cleanse like His shed blood! His blood so washed everything away that God forgot everything about it! What a perfect redemption!

Now, if God says He will remember your sins no more, who has the legal right to remind you of them? You may probably have been listening to a wrong person, for God through His Son's perfect sacrifice can't remember what you are trying to remind Him regarding your past that has been atoned for! Your ignorance is what is making you live in your past that doesn't exist anymore in the annals of God!

Please remember, these are the workings of God, not of man. God's very own works in and through His Son! (2Cor. 5:18)

Redemption Pictured In Jordan Crossing

Now, back to Jordan at the time that Israel crossed over it, for us to have a glimpse of the hidden works that transpired there!

Jordan is the second large-bodied mass of water that Israel had to cross in order to come into the Promised Land. Now this crossing prophetically points to our redemption which Jesus Christ has fulfilled for us.

And there is a prophetic methodology to this peculiar crossing.

"And it shall come to pass, as soon as the soles of the feet of the priests that bear the ark of <u>the LORD, the Lord of all the earth,</u> shall rest in the waters of Jordan, that the waters of Jordan shall be cut off from the waters that come down from above; and they shall stand upon an heap...

<u>And it came to pass</u>, when the people removed from their tents, to pass over Jordan, and the priests bearing the ark of the covenant before the people; And as they that bare the ark were come unto Jordan, and the feet of the priests that bare the ark were dipped in the brim of the water, (for Jordan overfloweth all his banks all the time of harvest,)

That the waters which came down from above stood and rose up upon an heap very far from the city Adam, that is beside Zaretan: and those that came down toward the sea of the plain, even the salt sea, failed, and were cut off: and the people passed over right against Jericho.

And the priests that bare the ark of the covenant of the LORD stood firm on dry ground in the midst of Jordan, and all the Israelites passed over on dry ground, until all the people were passed clean over Jordan." – Joshua 3:13-17.

From this all important scripture we can see that, there was a promise of what would happen when certain conditions are met. And when this was done, what the Lord had told them came to pass!

Scriptures informs us that as soon as the condition of the feet of **the priests** bearing the ark of the Lord of all the earth touched the waters that:

- *the waters which came down from above stood and rose up upon an heap.*
- *those [waters] that came down toward the sea of the plain, even the salt sea, failed, and*
- *those that came down toward the sea... were cut off.*

The Ark Bearing Priests

This is the first peculiarity about the crossing at Jordan.

According to the law of Moses, there are members of the Levitical priesthood set aside to transport the ark whenever Israel was on the move.

The family of the Kohathites, who were **Levites but not serving priests,** by divine order, had been assigned the great task of bearing the ark of the covenant – the symbol of God's presence.

"And the LORD spake unto Moses and unto Aaron, saying, Take the sum of the sons of Kohath from among the sons of Levi, after their families, by the house of their fathers, from thirty years old and upward even until fifty years old, all that enter into the host, to do the work in the tabernacle of the congregation.

This shall be the service of the sons of Kohath in the tabernacle of the congregation, about the most holy things: And when the camp setteth forward, Aaron shall come, and his sons, and they shall take down the covering vail, and cover the ark of testimony with it...

And when Aaron and his sons have made an end of covering the sanctuary, and all the vessels of the sanctuary, as the camp is to set forward; after that, the sons of Kohath shall come to bear it: but they shall not touch any holy thing, lest they die. These things are the burden of the sons of Kohath in the tabernacle of the congregation." – Numbers 4:1-5, 15.

If any other takes this task upon themselves it results in death, and the case of Uzzah in First Chronicles 13, readily comes to mind. That was why in First Chronicles 15, king David instructed that the right thing be done.

"And David called for Zadok and Abiathar the priests, and for the Levites, for Uriel, Asaiah, and Joel, Shemaiah, and Eliel, and Amminadab, And said unto them, Ye are the chief of the fathers of the Levites: sanctify yourselves, both ye and your brethren, that ye may bring up the ark of the LORD God of Israel unto the place that I have prepared for it. For because ye did it not at the first, the LORD our God made a breach upon us, for that we sought him not after the due order."
– I Chronicles 15:11-13.

However, because the occasion of **the crossing of Jordan, is peculiar, priests were instructed to bear the ark,** and it resulted in a miracle that remains a memorial for generations!

Addressing The LORD

Now, the addressing of the Lord God Jehovah as the Lord of all the earth in this place matters. The title refers to His ownership and Lordship of everything on the earth. And here, the Lord was simply exercising His right and authority on behalf of His children!

As prophesied by Moses, the Lord was going to cross Jordan ahead of them (Deuteronomy 31:2-3), and here is the fulfilment through the priest bearing the ark of His presence.

Through these priest, God stepped into the waters to make ways for His covenant people to cross into the place He had purchased for them for an inheritance!

With the covenant promise of dominion wherever the soles of their feet would come, God demonstrated this right of His on their behalf in the Jordan! Wherever you also stand today, because the Lord is with you, you shall not be swallowed up! What and where others dare not attempt, the Lord will make ways for you.

By these unprecedented supernatural works, we see that:

- *the priests... stood firm on dry ground in the midst of Jordan,*
- *all the Israelites passed over on dry ground, and*
- *all the people were passed clean over Jordan.*

The process of the failing of the waters from above, the cutting off of the waters that came down from Adam for the priests to stand on dry ground, and for the people of God to walk through the midst of Jordan on dry ground until all the people were "passed clean" over, is "very pregnant" with meanings!

This crossing over is a pointer to the works the Redeemer would accomplish on the cross of Calvary!

Additionally, archeologists who read this scripture made efforts to locate **"the city Adam"** mentioned in this scripture but found no physical place like that. This is because this city is a pointer to that which flowed spiritually from Adam downward to all men.

Remember, Romans 5:12 says, "For as by one man sin entered into the world and death by sin. So death passed upon all men for all have sinned"

The city Adam is not a physical place, as they came to discover but a spiritual reference point.

The flow of judgment from the first man, Adam, through his sin of disobedience and the breaking of covenant with God, **is what Christ came to cut off through His sacrifice at the cross!** Through the sacrifice of the Lamb of God, the sin and the consequences were atoned for hence the judgement ended there! The curse of the law, the sickness, and death were ended on that cross of the Lord Jesus Christ!

This cutting off of the waters is very crucial! Water represents life. The waters flowing from Adam, after his sin, was a death ridden life. It was not the true life God intended for man. The natural man is a living-dead creature.

And Jesus Chris declared that **He came that we might have life and to have it more abundantly!** (John 10:10) Now, come to think of it, He wouldn't have come to give us what we already possessed! That would be a waste of resources. But He actually came to give us the life from above and to separate us from the life below!

By His death, Jesus not only paid the price of redemption but also took our place being a man of sin for us, and thereby took the consequences, judgments or punishments of sin upon Himself! **By the divine exchange, He separated every believer from their pasts!**

As the Lamb slain from the foundation of the world, Jesus, through His death, went to the very root and beginning of things! He went to your beginning to correct the wrongs there! He went to deal with the root of sin!

Remember,

- He fulfilled the law (Matthew 5:17),
- He was made sin and condemned sin (2Cor. 5:21, Romans 8:3),
- He took our infirmities (Isaiah 53:3),
- He was made a curse (Galatians 3:13),
- He took our lack and poverty (2Cor. 8:9), and
- all the consequences of sin and our death (Hebrews 2:9)!

78

His was a complete work and a deliverance from the past and the root of unrighteousness!

"....The devil sinneth from the beginning. <u>For this purpose the Son of God was manifested</u>, that he might destroy [undo, reverse, paralyse, annul] the works of the devil." - I John 3:8 (Emphasis added).

What a heritage you have in Christ!

So, Jesus went to the beginning of things the very place where everything went wrong for man and creation and effected corrections there. That's why in His works He could heal a man born blind because He went to his past, before his blindness came, and reversed the works of the devil there because **Jesus is the beginning before the beginning!**

Whatever the enemy had conjured up before your problems manifested, the Lord has reversed in his redemption work! As you receive Him and the works He wrought by faith today, He is effecting the same in your life for a testimony!

Whatever wisdom the enemy had engaged against you before you were married, which is now working against your joy and peace, whatever existed before you which is the hidden reason behind your predicament, Jesus went deep down to touch those things and has reversed them! You are delivered! (John 8:36)

Oh, what a Saviour Christ is! What a salvation is ours!

Because He went and touched the root of things, this is why when we got born again, our lives were made new as if we had never sinned!

The root of your issues, by His blood and perfect sacrifice, withers today, now, in the perfect name of Jesus Christ!

You are by His perfect sacrifice separated from that generational curse that has ravaged your biological lineage! That evil cycle of misfortune ends now, in the name of Jesus Christ!

What has been conquered for you has no more power over your life! Everything you therefore resist henceforth in His knowledge, in His name and power of His sacrifice shall give way for you to go forward!

God has reached right back to your past, in and through His Son, to the things that happened before your naming ceremony, wedding, your journey… to the secret things done to arrest your life and destiny, and reversed them!

Remember, the Holy Spirit came as a promise and fruit of what Christ has wrought. And He searches all things, even deep, hidden and secret things to bring about the testimony of Jesus Christ in your life thereby making you a living witness! (ICor. 2:9-10, Acts 1:8). The Holy Spirit is here to glorify Jesus Christ in your life!

By His sacrifice, through the blood of His cross, God has purged and reconciled all things unto Himself. (Colossians1:21). Before men could be reconciled unto God, their sins and the consequences had to be dealt with. And this was what Jesus did on the cross, typified in the crossing over of Jordan by Israel.

Irreversible Death Blow!

The work of redemption covered all grounds, both spiritual and physical! Not only are we changed in our spirit and made new but also **our bodies shall be changed as part of the consummate work in the end.** When Christ was raised from death, it was a bodily resurrection, and not just spiritual!

"But is now made manifest by the appearing of our Saviour Jesus Christ, who hath abolished death, and hath brought life and immortality to light through the gospel." – 2 Timothy 1:10.

When the waters failed from Adam, the death life ceased to flow into the life of everyone that received the work of redemption in Christ. Over such class of people, death has no final say again! With all authority in heaven and on earth in the hands of Jesus our Saviour, nothing outside Him can ever have dominion or final say anymore!

By His perfect sacrifice, Jesus dealt an irrecoverable blow to death over His own! Hear Him declare with all verity:

"Verily, verily, I say unto you, <u>He that heareth my word, and believeth</u> on him that sent me, hath everlasting life, and shall not come into condemnation; but <u>is</u> passed from death unto life. Verily, verily, I say unto you, The hour is coming, and now is, when the dead shall hear the voice of the Son of God: and they that hear shall live.

For as the Father hath life in himself; so hath he given to the Son to have life in himself; And hath given him authority to execute judgment also, because he is the Son of man.

81

Marvel not at this: for the hour is coming, in the which all that are in the graves shall hear his voice, And shall come forth; they that have done good, unto the resurrection of life; and they that have done evil, unto the resurrection of damnation"
-John 5:24-29.

As practically demonstrated in Lazarus, when the Lord Jesus called out to Lazarus, death and whatever killed him gave up on him and he that was dead came forth!

Now by Jesus, death died! Over His own, He has abolished death!

Another demonstration, though prophetically, is in Ezekiel 37 wherein the very dry bones of the slain ones came back to life a living army! He is Lord forever over death!

As sin shall not have dominion over you, death cannot and shall not have dominion over you!

This is why through the baptism of John in Jordan, Christ brought into light the deep, mysterious and wonderful works of redemption!

The Waters of the Beginning - Genesis!

Let's touch one more thing about waters, and this is found right there in the book of beginnings!

You see, there are two things in the book of Genesis chapter one, during the process of creation by God **that were never stated or concluded with this phrase:**

82

"And God saw... that it was good." – *Genesis 1:4.*

One of those things has to do with the waters, the separation of the waters.

"And God said, Let there be a firmament in the midst of the waters, and let it divide the waters from the waters. And God made the firmament, and divided the waters which were under the firmament from the waters which were above the firmament: and it was so. And God called the firmament Heaven. And the evening and the morning were the second day. And God said, Let the waters under the heaven be gathered together unto one place, and let the dry land appear: and it was so." – *Genesis 1:6-9.*

This passage informs us of two bodies of waters. In order to put distinction between them, God had to do something. There was a permanent fixture, **firm-a-ment**, in the midst of the waters to divide the waters above from the waters beneath!

Beloved, there are things that look alike but must not be mixed together! God is holy and therefore hate mixtures! We see His holiness in principle here.

If you travel by water today and get to the point where the Atlantic ocean and the Pacific ocean meet, you will see a distinction between the two. There is no mixing at all! It's still one of the wonders of God till date!

Beloved, there are waters and there are waters. May your life, by the blood of Jesus Christ, be forever separated from the wrong waters! Whatever looks innocent but is geared towards polluting your life, the Lord will separate you from them and separate them from you!

In the book of Revelation, from the throne of God and the Lamb, flows water from the river of life! This water represent the life of the Holy Spirit, and the blessings of redemption which the One sitting on the throne secured for those who believed and received Him! The waters are for them to drink and manifest supernatural fruits!

"And he shewed me a pure river of water of life, clear as crystal, proceeding out of the throne of God and of the Lamb."
– Revelation 22:1.

When you read other accounts of what the Lamb would accomplish and give to those who follow Him, you will appreciate the fact that the water of the river of life is often in the plural! Among countless scriptures please read Isaiah 35:1-7, Ezekiel 47:1-12, Zechariah 14:8, John 7:37-38, Revelation 7:17.

Therefore, from His throne He sends His water continually to water those connected to Him! And the effects are very visible in the trees on the banks of that river! (Rev. 22:2-3)

There is a life from above, and there is a life from beneath symbolized by waters. And except you are born from above, you cannot see nor enter into the kingdom of God. That which is born from above is far different from that which is born below! Jesus came that we might be born from above and be delivered from that which is beneath!

"Jesus answered, Verily, verily, I say unto thee, <u>Except</u> a man be born of water and of the Spirit, he cannot enter into the kingdom of God. That which is born of the flesh is flesh; and that which is born of the Spirit is spirit. Marvel not that I said unto thee, Ye must be born again." – John 3:5-7.

So, baptism is simply a symbol of that which God has wrought, and it works for those who believe and receive Jesus Christ into their lives as Lord and Saviour!

You don't get born again by being baptized in water. You are simply by faith identifying and showing evidence or testifying to what Christ has wrought for you and to also key-in to enjoy the blessings of redemption!

The Raised Man – The New Man – The Son of God!

"...But they regard not the work of the LORD, neither consider the operation of his hands. Therefore my people are gone into captivity, because they have no knowledge: and their honourable men are famished, and their multitude dried up with thirst." – Isaiah 5:12b-13.

Now let's look back again at the works of redemption wrought at Jordan. The reason we are looking at these things is to know the treasures that redemption holds for us and begin to live in them. Therefore, captivity due to the lack of knowledge ends over your life today, and your life shall no more be out of course with God! (Psalm 82:5-6).

> *"Our old history ends with the cross, our new history begins with His resurrection"* – Watchman Nee

You need to understand that the man who came out of that Jordan water was a clean man, a man with no sin in God's sight. He is the man whose sins and iniquities God remembers no more for judgement has been passed upon him! The man God raised anew from these waters is His man! He has brought forth beauty out of ashes! He is another man entirely, created after His righteousness and true holiness! (Ephesians 4:24).

Those who come to Christ through His atonement have their sins forgiven that God remembers them no more, and therefore begins a new work in that man.

Will God raise a sinner? If His eyes are too pure to behold iniquity, how will He by His right hand touch and raise a sinner?! No! This new man is a blessed man. The man of God's very blessing! This is who you are in Christ!

The man who went into the waters of Jordan was not the same man who came out of the same waters! **Jordan, spiritually speaking, represents the grave and a womb** -a place of burial of the old man and a place of birth of the new man!

In the same water, within the space of a few seconds of baptism, we have two different men, spiritually speaking! That's the wonder of redemption! **There was a man dead in sins and trespasses and there is a man forgiven all his sins and trespasses Baptism shows us the transition from one humanity to another!**

"And you, being dead in your sins and the uncircumcision of your flesh, hath he quickened together with him, having forgiven you all trespasses." – Colossians 2:13.

86

The man who went into Jordan was sentenced to death because of sin and buried there. There the first man ended through sin, buried out of God's sight. The man who came out of the water was God's new man, His raised man. He is the man raised into newness of life! The man God to whom inputs no sin!

"Even as David also describeth the blessedness of the man, unto whom God imputeth righteousness without works, Saying, Blessed are they whose iniquities are forgiven, and whose sins are covered." – Romans 4:6-7.

This time, the sins are not just covered but they have been blotted out by a perfect sacrifice of Jesus Christ. Cut off, removed by the blood of His cross. This is God's blessed man!

A Glimpse at the Beginning!

Now, you will also do well to remember that when He was coming out of the water, there was an unprecedented scene as we had it in the beginning, right in the book of Genesis but with a slight difference.

"And Jesus, when he was baptized, went up straightway out of the water: and, lo, the heavens were opened unto him, and he saw the Spirit of God descending like a dove, and lighting upon him: And lo a voice from heaven, saying, This is my beloved Son, in whom I am well pleased." – Matthew 3:16-17.

In the case of the new man or the man with a new beginning, we see the Holy Ghost appearing as at the beginning – when

87

the Spirit of God hovered upon the waters. Not only so, as prophesied in Daniel 9:24, that after the perfect sacrifice, the anointing of that which is holy will be the next phase!

"And the earth was without form, and void; and darkness was upon the face of the deep. And the Spirit of God moved upon the face of the waters." - Genesis 1:2.

The Holy Ghost, who was hovering over the waters at the beginning, showed up again upon the man who came out of these waters of Jordan! His quickening and divine enabling power came upon Him whom God has raised!

In the beginning, the Spirit of God only hovered over the waters and found no place of rest. However, this time, in this brand new beginning of man, He didn't disappear out of the scene but descended upon this man! And **God by His Spirit, has found the man of His pleasing, the man of His rest!**

There is a total change from the former here; God has found rest with His man! Can you now see the depth of the richness and riches of your redemption in Christ? You are chosen of His and anointed!

"Concerning his Son Jesus Christ our Lord, which was made of the seed of David according to the flesh; And declared to be the Son of God with power, according to the spirit of holiness, by the resurrection from the dead." - Romans 1:3-4.

This new man has been created after God – in the image of God and His holiness!

88

"And that ye put on the new man, which after God is created in righteousness and true holiness."- Ephesians 4:24.

Remember, Jesus kept declaring Himself the Son of man, even though he is the Son of God. But for the work of redeeming man, He put on the title as the Son of man. **And when was Jesus declared the Son of God?** Yes, when He was raised from the waters! - a foreshadowing of the time when He will be raised from the dead!

Remember Israel's case when they crossed over that it was written: *"...all the people were passed clean over Jordan." - Joshua 3:17.*

The Message version of the Bible puts it this way: *"...Finally the whole nation was across Jordan, and not one wet foot." -Joshua 3:17 (MSG - The Message Bible)*

As Israel went through Jordan, the waters were so totally cut off that not a single drop or wetness stuck to or with them! They all came out pure! All, not a few!

You have been cleansed by the blood of the Lamb from every sin and filth of sin. You have no business with sin again. The man whom God raised was a clean man. Cleansed from every filthiness of the spirit. You can never come out of Jordan by yourself, but this is God's work!

Look again at God's conversation with Peter in this regard which underscores what God has wrought in the new man:

"And saw heaven opened, and a certain vessel descending unto him, as it had been a great sheet knit at the four corners, and let

down to the earth: Wherein were all manner of fourfooted beasts of the earth, and wild beasts, and creeping things, and fowls of the air.

And there came a voice to him, Rise, Peter; kill, and eat. But Peter said, Not so, Lord; for I have never eaten any thing that is common or unclean. And the voice spake unto him again the second time, <u>What God hath cleansed, that call not thou common.</u> This was done thrice: and the vessel was received up again into heaven." - Acts 10:11-16.

Christ – Raised Clean Man!

"...all the people were passed clean over Jordan." - Joshua 3:17.

Perhaps we need to understand this part of the Jordan works a little bit more just for emphasis. It's more than saying all or the entirety of the people, with none left behind, went over Jordan. The word **"clean"** here has depth in it!

The finished work of Christ on the cross cannot be overlooked or over emphasized. It's a tremendous work. It may sound like repetition but it's not. The word "clean" here holds the keys to the great riches and richness of redemption works.

The going down of Jesus Christ into the Jordan waters, which is a pointer to His going to the cross, is worth being closely looked at, over and over again, in order to understand or comprehend what went down with Him or that He took down with Him.

The reason being that scriptures tell us that He took unto Himself our sins, griefs, sorrows, infirmities, etc. And we have to see that ALL He took down into the waters or took upon Himself on the cross, never rose with Him at resurrection!

When Christ rose from the dead, just like Lazarus, there was no smell or trace of decomposition in Him. Whatever overpowered and killed Lazarus gave up on him at the voice of the Lord who Himself is the Resurrection and Life!

On the cross, Jesus bore all our sickness, took on Himself our curses, pain, griefs… all that came with sin. All these things went into the grave with Him as a condemned man. However, when He would be raised from the dead, none of those things rose with Him! He came out a clean Man!

All sicknesses, known and unknown, all the curses, all the pains… everything the enemy has ever or could ever bring about through sin on man never rose out from the grave with Jesus Christ! This is the "clean" passing over.

The man who came out from the water was a curseless and uncursable Man! This is what Christ did for you!

"__Surely__ he hath borne our griefs, and carried our sorrows: yet we did esteem him stricken, smitten of God, and afflicted. But he was wounded for our transgressions, he was bruised for our iniquities: the chastisement of our peace was upon him; and with his stripes we are healed." – Isaiah 53:4-5.

When Christ rose from the dead, the mark of nails in His hands and the wound in His side were the only things similar between the one who went to the cross and the one who rose

91

from death. And those marks are there for a purpose, as a witness of the work done!

> *"After death something new begins, over which all powers of the world of death have no more might."*
> *- Dietrich Bonhoeffer*

Therefore what He carried and buried in Jordan, you are not permitted to carry in your life again! Ever! Sickness, affliction, poverty, curses… are no more your load and lot! You have every right in Christ Jesus to reject them. What He hath borne is no more your burden!

He has tasted death for you, therefore premature death is not your lot!

Why should generational curses continue to operate in your life? Why should evil cycle continue to hold over your life? Your case is now different and you should stand on that! You are uncursable!

"Herein is our love made perfect, that we may have boldness in the day of judgment: because as he is, so are we in this world." *– I John 4:17.*

Remember, *"as He is so are we in this world,"* not till we get to heaven. There is a spiritual likeness here and now. As long as we live and walk in the Spirit, we have the right to enjoy all His provisions.

Now, can Christ be made sick again? Can He go back to the cross and carry curses again? Therefore, whatever can't harass Him now has no right or authority to happen over your life! You can live a sickness free, curse free, poverty free life! It's part of the choices you have made in redemption. It's your right for you to exercise!

Remember, in His parable of the sower while some grounds had nothing to show for the sown word of the Kingdom, some brought forth thirty, some sixty and some hundred folds. There is therefore room for you to grow consistently and enjoy exceedingly more than you are now as you engage His knowledge!

"But the path of the just is as the shining light, that shineth more and more unto the perfect day." - Proverbs 4:18.

By the Light of Life, you can yet reach farther, go over and beyond, rise higher, be greater and shine brighter than ever in the glory of the grace of redemption as you engage His knowledge!

The Man of Another Law - The Law of The Spirit

"...The waters which came down from above stood and rose up upon an heap very far from the city Adam, that is beside Zaretan: and those that came down toward the sea of the plain, even the salt sea, failed, and were cut off: and the people passed over right against Jericho." - Joshua 3:17.

For the people to pass over right against Jericho, the waters which came down stood and rose up as a heap. This is an amazing work of our God. With these waters being made into a heap, the people walked through Jordan on a dry ground.

Mind you, it was not wet ground but dry ground right in the midst of Jordan!

The forming of a heap of waters was the operation of another law. That **"law"** kept the water from running down and sweeping away the people in the midst of the river, it also made sure not a drop of the waters stuck with the people while they walked through. This is the law of the Spirit!

When Jesus walked on water, He wasn't violating any law, He simply engaged a higher law that kept Him afloat. This is the case also in the crossing of Jordan, a miracle of dryness in the midst of the waters.

This is like the case of Goshen in the midst of Egypt. Whatever was being suffered in the whole of Egypt, the case was different in Goshen even though it was in Egypt. The God of distinction hasn't changed!

In Christ Jesus, we have His life such that right in the midst of this world we are kept by another law that annuls or preserves us from the law of sin and death!

Sin is present in the world, but it has no power over believers walking in Christ! They are not subject to sin. They are not slave to sin. The one who is *"born of God sinneth not!"* (I John 5:18)

"There is therefore now no condemnation to them which are in Christ Jesus, who walk not after the flesh, but after the Spirit. <u>For the law of the Spirit of life in Christ Jesus hath made me free from the law of sin and death.</u>

For what the law could not do, in that it was weak through the flesh, God sending his own Son in the likeness of sinful flesh, and for sin, condemned sin in the flesh: That the righteousness of the law might be fulfilled in us, who walk not after the flesh, but after the Spirit." – Romans 8:1-4.

As long as Israel was walking through Jordan, the waters could not come down on them because the feet of the priests bearing the ark of the covenant of God was still standing in Jordan. As our High Priest, when we abide in Christ, walking after the Spirit, we are preserved from the power of sin in the world!

"For sin shall not have dominion over you: for ye are not under the law, but under grace." – Romans 6:14.

The Man of New Beginning

"Who is the image of the invisible God, the firstborn of every creature." – Colossians 1:15.

> *"The risen life of Jesus Christ is the nourishment and strengthening and blessing and life of a Christian."*
> *-Alexandar Maclaren.*

Our discourse in this book will be incomplete without touching something about our Lord's title, which is a pointer to His position in God's scheme of things. It is of utmost importance that believers understand to the deepest level revealed or permitted by God in the process of their salvation.

Our Lord would have us rooted and built up in Him, and thereby abound unto all good works!

95

"As ye have therefore received Christ Jesus the Lord, so walk ye in him: Rooted and built up in him, and stablished in the faith, as ye have been taught, abounding therein with thanksgiving."
– Colossians 2:6-7.

We therefore need to still touch an aspect of the coming out of the waters of Jordan that every believer in Christ needs to clearly understand. This will gladden the new believer, reinforce his/her faith and strengthen the resolve of the older faithfuls.

We have earlier stated that Jordan represent a grave and a womb. It represents the place of burial of the old man, the man contaminated with sin and everything about him. And at the same time, it's the place of the birth of the new man whom God raised by the life giving action of the Holy Spirit.

This coming out of the waters is the new beginning of the newly created man.

Now, looking at the titles and the position of God's Son in creation, you will see that the first place belong to Him. It's His natural place. It's His by right and nature. No one can take that from Him. However, not only the first place in terms of position but more importantly the instrument for the creation of every other creature.

You see, in creation, everything God made He did so through the Son.

"In the beginning was the Word, and the Word was with God, and the Word was God. The same was in the beginning with God. All things were made by him; and without him was not any thing made that was made." – John 1:1-3.

96

Therefore when Jesus came, as God's principle of and in creation is, He began to do everything in and through Jesus Christ His Son. Whatever therefore is not through the Son, it is not of God!

Egypt's Firstborn Saga!

"For if the firstfruit be holy, the lump is also holy: and if the root be holy, so are the branches." – Romans 11:16.

By the spiritual law of firsts, the firstborn or firstfruit determines the course of things in that which follows. God's place is first in His creation, and in line with this, He asks that all firstborn, and firstfruits belong to Him. The disobedience to this demand, this right of God, is what caused irreversible havoc in Egypt that made them let Israel go!

The Lord made a demand in Egypt for that which belonged to Him – the firstborn of all things, man and beast. All that opens the womb or matrix are the Lord's – they belong to Him as His right in all creation. It's non-negotiable else an imbalance will ensue! The Lord came to pass-over Egypt to receive what is His due.

Now, upon the houses or homes where the blood of the Passover lamb, representing that which belonged to God, was not seen was visited by the destroyer who came to claim what is the Lord's own – all the firstborn ones!

"Because all the firstborn are mine; for on the day that I smote all the firstborn in the land of Egypt I hallowed unto me all the firstborn in Israel, both man and beast: mine shall they be: I am the LORD." – Numbers 3:13.

Please, remember what the demand in Egypt was –

"And thou shalt say unto Pharaoh, Thus saith the LORD, Israel is my son, even <u>my firstborn</u>: And I say unto thee, <u>Let my son go, that he may serve me</u>: and if thou refuse to let him go, behold, I will slay thy son, even thy firstborn." – Exodus 4:22-23.

There are two things in this scripture. Israel is God's Son, His firstborn, and they stand to represent the first in creation as every first of animal or man in creation are the Lord's right. **The wisdom of the Egyptians failed them in this case as they held unto what belonged to God Almighty!**

And at the end of the day, as the Lord said, He came to demand and receive that which is His due among all creation! And as nothing could stop Him from receiving His due, all the firstborn of man and beast were taken, in the homes where His instruction was not complied with, as the Lord passed-over Egypt!

In their wisdom, they became foolish, and lost everything. This is how the foolishness of preaching is designed to confound those who say they are wise!

Now, every believer in Christ is a firstborn one through Jesus Christ, and therefore those who touch you touch disaster! As those who refused His demand in Egypt were not found guiltless, and therefore paid dearly, those who hold onto your life and destiny and shall not be guiltless!

"Israel was holiness unto the LORD, and the firstfruits of his increase: all that devour him shall offend; evil shall come upon them, saith the LORD." – Jeremiah 2:3.

"For I am the LORD thy God, the Holy One of Israel, thy Saviour: I gave Egypt for thy ransom, Ethiopia and Seba for thee. Since thou wast precious in my sight, thou hast been honourable, and I have loved thee: therefore will I give men for thee, and people for thy life." – Isaiah 43:3-4.

Check through the scriptures, no one has ever touched Israel and remained the same. At the end of the day, disaster overtook them. In fact, some of them were swept out of existence! The same applies to those who tamper with every believer in Christ today.

Even Satan who touched the Lamb of God lost everything he had ever stolen from man through deception! He touched a wrong Man, and lost all he ever acquired! **Your enemies shall suffer irrecoverable losses!** Henceforth, you're a bad market for every adversary!

This World and That World!

We shall do well to understand that there is a new order of things in God's new creation. As it was in the beginning before the foundation of the world, the Son has simply come again, stepping out of eternity, to lead and become the foundation and the instrument of creation of and for the new order.

This is why everything finds explanation in Christ Jesus. Everything! **He is the heir of all things.** Without Him, there is nothing!

"In the beginning was the Word, and the Word was with God, and the Word was God. The same was in the beginning with God. All things were made by him; and without him was not any thing made that was made." – John 1:1-3.

"Who is the image of the invisible God, <u>the firstborn of every creature</u>: For by him were all things created, that are in heaven, and that are in earth, visible and invisible, whether they be thrones, or dominions, or principalities, or powers: all things were created by him, and for him: And he is before all things, and by him all things consist."
- Colossians 1:15-17.

He is before all things. Before Abraham was, He had been! (John 8:58). He had a glory with the Father before the world began (John 17:5). He had existed before anything, and by Him, everything has its being. This is the position of the firstborn!

"And Jesus answering said unto them, The children of <u>this world</u> marry, and are given in marriage: But they which shall be accounted <u>worthy to obtain that world</u>, and the resurrection from the dead, neither marry, nor are given in marriage:"
- Luke 20:34.

From our Lord's statement, there is a new world in the horizon. A new heaven and earth, a world to come is in view, and the works concerning that world has begun. There are thus men in this present world or age that at the end of the day would be accounted worthy to obtain that world or age to come. The Son came because of them that would be accounted worthy to obtain that world.

Through redemption, He's taking people out, as in Egypt, to that which He has purchased by His sacrifice – the world to come! (Hebrews 2:5). This is the heart of the Gospel!

"Forasmuch then as the children are partakers of flesh and blood, he also himself likewise took part of the same; that through death he might destroy him that had the power of death, that is, the devil; And deliver them who through fear of death were all their lifetime subject to bondage.

For verily he took not on him the nature of angels; but he took on him the seed of Abraham. Wherefore in all things it behoved him to be made like unto his brethren, that he might be a merciful and faithful high priest in things pertaining to God, to make reconciliation for the sins of the people."
–Hebrews 2:14-17.

This scripture clearly shows the reason for incarnation, why the Son of God stepped out of eternity into time, in flesh and blood to bring men out into the full plan of salvation.

Therefore, because God is raising sons unto Himself in this present age for the world or ages to come, the Son came out from the bosom of the Father to lead the new creation and be the instrument for everything in it just as it was. The principle hasn't changed. His title as the firstborn of all creation is still the same!

Even from the parables of our Lord Jesus Christ, it is so glaring how far He would go for His own, what price he would pay just for one soul!

"Again, the kingdom of heaven is like unto <u>treasure hid in a field</u>; the which when a man hath found, he hideth, and for joy thereof goeth and selleth all that he hath, and <u>buyeth that field.</u>

Again, the kingdom of heaven is like unto a merchant man, seeking goodly pearls: Who, when he had found one pearl of great price, went and sold all that he had, and bought it."
–Matthew 13:44-46.

Now consider, with this scripture in mind, what is written in Philippians 2:6-8, and you will see the steps Jesus took to purchase men out of this world unto Himself!

"Who, being in the form of God, thought it not robbery to be equal with God: But made himself of no reputation, and took upon him the form of a servant, and was made in the likeness of men:

And being found in fashion as a man, he humbled himself, and became obedient unto death, even the death of the cross."
– Philippians 2:6-8.

The children, who are partakers of flesh and blood, are the treasures hidden in the field. You, yes you, are that peculiar treasure He came for! He sold everything to purchase the field that holds you! He traded everything to redeem you out from the world back unto Himself! That field is the world.

Therefore for that purpose, it is written that *"in all things it behoved him to be made like unto his brethren"*, He humbled Himself and *"and was made in the likeness of men"* for the suffering of death to deliver them out from death!

You are the reason He became a man. You are the treasure He came to purchase out of the world. Jesus Christ didn't die for the world, He purchased the world because you are in it! (Matthew 13:44). Is that not why we are asked not to love the world? (I John 2:15). It's because he loved the world because you are in it!

Jesus Christ did not originally exist in the likeness of men but was made now in the likeness of men to come into what men had come into, so that He can bring into who and what He is!

The second parable deals with a pearl for which He sold all He had to purchase. Pearls are gems or treasures buried deep in the sea. **The two parables therefore touched on deeps in the earth and sea – the place Jesus Christ went in His death for the redemption of mankind!** These parables are clearly about the extent the Lord would go to redeem one soul, you!

He had one life and gave it up for you! So why would you sell off when your worth is beyond rubies, dollars and pounds? If your life is valued as much as the blood of the Son of God, then your value is beyond, measure! Begin to carry a sense of worth and value henceforth!

Consider His High Priestly prayer –

"I have manifested thy name unto the men which thou gavest me out of the world: thine they were, and thou gavest them me; and they have kept thy word. Now they have known that all things whatsoever thou hast given me are of thee... I pray for them: I pray not for the world, but for them which thou hast given me; for they are thine. And all mine are thine, and thine are mine; and I am glorified in them." - John 17:6-10.

103

He prayed for those of His in the world not the world. This is a personal God, Who would do anything for His own! Have you heard of any other God anywhere who has ever done or will ever do this for His own? No other God except Jehovah! (Deut. 4:32-34).And there is no god beside Him!

"What man of you, having an hundred sheep, if he lose one of them, doth not leave the ninety and nine in the wilderness, and go after that which is lost, until he find it?

And when he hath found it, he layeth it on his shoulders, rejoicing. And when he cometh home, he calleth together his friends and neighbours, saying unto them, Rejoice with me; for I have found my sheep which was lost. I say unto you, that likewise joy shall be in heaven over one sinner that repenteth, more than over ninety and nine just persons, which need no repentance." – Luke 15:4-7.

The Lord stripped Himself and left everything behind that made Him God and took on the likeness of men, your likeness! **Even though He was rich, yet for your sake He became poor so that through His poverty, you might be rich!** (2Cor. 8:9). What a God! You, yes you, are the reason He became man! **Look at the extent He went just because of you only!**

This is why **Christianity does not stand in the same class with any other religion, no matter how good they may seem to be!** It's simply exceptional in everything and on every ground! What a glorious God we serve!

The Son therefore took on flesh and blood that through death He may destroy him who wielded the power of death and thereby lead men out of the bondage of the fear of death into life eternal. He came to open the door out of this creation into the new creation!

The Leading Lamb!

"And he is before all things, and by him all things consist ...the beginning, the firstborn from the dead; THAT IN ALL THINGS he might have the PREEMINENCE."
– Colossians 1:17-18.

"A dead Christ I must do everything for; a living Christ does everything for me!"
- Andrew Murray

As in Egypt with the Passover lamb,
He came to redeem out of the world a peculiar people, open the door to lead God's sons unto the city which hath foundations whose builder and maker is God!

The powers of the present age are not great enough to stop the operations of the world to come. He came to take preeminence, to take the lead - the true and original lead ahead of anything and everything.

Jesus Christ had been before sin came. He had existed with the Father before sickness, death, satan, principalities, powers… ever came into being. So He stepped out of eternity to take the lead and the place that belongs to Him alone, His rightful place, and then in taking pre-eminence, lead out those who believe, receive and follow Him!

He therefore became poor, to arrest, paralyse and destroy the power of poverty over those who believe and received Him.

He was made sin to deliver and set free from the penalty of sin, preserve from the power of sin and protect from the presence of sin!

This is why salvation is often in scriptures written in three tenses indicating that **we have been saved, we are being saved, and we shall be saved!** (Ephesians 2:5, I Cor. 1:18, Mark 13:13).

Jesus took on flesh and blood, become as we are to deliver us from what we are that we might become as He is and reign in and with Him.

"He came unto his own, and his own received him not. But as many as received him, to them gave he power to become the sons of God, even to them that believe on his name: Which were born, not of blood, nor of the will of the flesh, nor of the will of man, but of God." - John 1:11-13.

"Herein is our love made perfect, that we may have boldness in the day of judgment: because as he is, so are we in this world."
- I John 4:17.

Having entered into all things that man could ever enter into, in his sinful state, and taken pre-eminence, nothing shall hold you bound again! Not even death or the grave! Jesus entered into death and came out, even took enough time to fold the napkins with which His head was wrapped during burial! He entered in and took pre-eminence!

So the day He calls, as He called Lazarus, those who believe in Him, and those who died or slept in Him, shall wake up and be reclaimed back unto Him. No death shall be able to stop them for Jesus Himself is the resurrection and Life!

106

As He is still at work, speaking (John 5:19), may you hear His voice today and come out of every evil hold over your life and destiny!

"For as the Father raiseth up the dead, and quickeneth them; even so the Son quickeneth whom he will. For the Father judgeth no man, but hath committed all judgment unto the Son: That all men should honour the Son, even as they honour the Father. He that honoureth not the Son honoureth not the Father which hath sent him.

Verily, verily, I say unto you, He that heareth my word, and believeth on him that sent me, hath everlasting life, and shall not come into condemnation; but is passed from death unto life. Verily, verily, I say unto you, The hour is coming, and now is, when the dead shall hear the voice of the Son of God: and they that hear shall live. For as the Father hath life in himself; so hath he given to the Son to have life in himself...

Marvel not at this: for the hour is coming, in the which all that are in the graves shall hear his voice, And shall come forth; they that have done good, unto the resurrection of life; and they that have done evil, unto the resurrection of damnation."
–John 5:21-29.

Therefore by taking pre-eminence, He has opened the door out of every situation and circumstance for you! Your prison doors are open! Your way out of debt, sickness and curses are wide open! He opened the way out from death. As the keys are still in His hand, He won't allow you to be held down by their power!

> *"Our God is for us a God of salvation; his are the ways out of death." –Psalm 68:20 (BBE)*

107

"He that is our God is the God of salvation; and unto GOD the Lord belong the issues from death."-Psalm 68:20 (KJV)

"Our *God is the *God of salvation; and with Jehovah, the Lord, are the goings forth even from death." –Psalm 68:20 (Darby).

"God Himself is to us a God for deliverances, And Jehovah Lord hath the outgoings of death." –Psalm 68:20 (YLT).

"I am he that liveth, and was dead; and, behold, I am alive for evermore, Amen; and have the keys of hell and of death." – Revelations 1:18.

"The Resurrection and Life" has taken pre-eminence, He wields the keys of death and hell and therefore, the bondage of the fear of death is forever broken over your life! Nothing good withers from your hand nor dies off your life again!

By His works of salvation, He has opened the way out of every situation and circumstance. **Those things you are going through now can never have the final say in your affairs again!** This day forward, you're coming out from that darkness, dungeon, trap, sickness, lack, poverty, and every evil siege!

Remember, at the beginning of His Gospel, He came to declare freedom and to open doors –

"And there was delivered unto him the book of the prophet Esaias. And when he had opened the book, he found the place where it was written,

The Spirit of the Lord is upon me, because he hath anointed me to preach the gospel to the poor; he hath sent me to heal the brokenhearted, to preach deliverance to the captives, and recovering of sight to the blind, to set at liberty them that are bruised, To preach the acceptable year of the Lord.

And he closed the book, and he gave it again to the minister, and sat down. And the eyes of all them that were in the synagogue were fastened on him. And he began to say unto them, This day is this scripture fulfilled in your ears." - Luke 4:17-21.

This scripture is already fulfilled, so what are you still doing at the same spot all these years? Get up and walk!

The Omnipresent Saviour!

"For where two or three are gathered together in my name, there am I in the midst of them." - Matthew 18:20.

We shall do well to touch another scripture that spoke vividly of His going down into lower part of the earth for the purpose that He might take pre-eminence in all things. We are simply making every attempt to understand and to stand in the light of our exceptional redemption!

"Wherefore he saith, When he ascended up on high, he led captivity captive, and gave gifts unto men. (Now that he ascended, what is it but that he also descended first into the lower parts of the earth? He that descended is the same also that ascended up far above all heavens, that he might fill all things.)" - Ephesians 4:8-10.

The death and burial of our Lord Jesus Christ, as foreshadowed in the water baptism, as also revealed in scriptures, makes us understand the process and the fruits of His travails for our salvation.

Now, there is a given promise by the Lord in the Book of Matthew that He will be everywhere and anywhere men would gather unto His name (Matthew 18:20). This promise, as part of the salvation package which must be fulfilled, forms one of the reasons He had to go down into the belly of the earth, and be raised above the heavens.

As stated in Ephesians 4:8-10, Jesus went into the lower parts of the earth and was raised higher than the heavens THAT He might fill all things! As Lord over all creation, He is now everywhere. He fills the whole of the universe.

"For such an high priest became us, who is holy, harmless, undefiled, separate from sinners, and made higher than the heavens." – Hebrews 7:26.

Now, there's nowhere men will call upon His name that He will not answer. **In the desert, ocean, seas, lakes, caves, mountain tops... He is there and shows up at the mention or gathering unto of His great name because He now fills all things.** For it pleased the Father that in Him should all fullness dwell!

"For it pleased the Father that in him should all fullness dwell."
– Colossians 1:19.

You are therefore never without access or connection to His help, anywhere you may be! As promised, He will never leave you nor forsake you! (Hebrews 13:5). Through redemption, you will never walk alone again!

Right in the waters, fires or whatever you may be passing through now, you are not alone! And because He is with you, He shall bring you out better! (Job 23:10)

"When thou passest through the waters, I will be with thee; and through the rivers, they shall not overflow thee: when thou walkest through the fire, thou shalt not be burned; neither shall the flame kindle upon thee." – Isaiah 43:2.

Shalom!

CHAPTER FIVE

Jonah's Big Fish

―――――――⟨❦⟩―――――――

*"It is a fact that the Lord Jesus has
already died for you. It is also a fact that you have
already died with the Lord Jesus.*

*If you do not believe in your death with Christ,
you will not be able to receive the effectiveness of
death with Him – freedom from sin."*

- Watchman Nee

The Son and Sound

"God, who at sundry times and in divers manners spake in time past unto the fathers by the prophets, Hath in these last days spoken unto us by his Son, whom he hath appointed heir of all things, by whom also he made the worlds." - Hebrews 1:1-2.

Right from the old times, God had always spoken to His people, employing many means at different times to speak. Looking at the Old Testament scriptures, it will be discovered that God spoke by words and also by acts. This scripture informs that the means through which God spoke was "diverse".

However, in these end times, God has chosen to speak in just one all-inclusive way! He is speaking only in and by His Son Jesus Christ. God has gathered all His "speakings" into Him. He is God's voice personalized! (Matthew 17:5).

Therefore, whatever is outside of Him is not from God! It's that straight forward! Christ is the all-inclusive way of hearing from God. And in Him is all that God ever wants to say!

When you look at the Son, you see God speaking. All He ever spoke even in the olden days and Old Testament had parts and portions in the Son. But in these last times, the Father gathered everything together in Him! Therefore, **be mindful who you heed, if it's not found in Christ, it's far from God!**

Now, let's explore some things around one of the ways God spoke in the times past.

The Sound of Signs

"The heavens declare the glory of God; and the firmament sheweth his handywork. Day unto day uttereth speech, and night unto night sheweth knowledge. There is no speech nor language, where their voice is not heard." – Psalm 19:1-3 (KJV).

Everything in life is built with ears to hear for they are products of the word, God's word. We all are children or products of that which God spoke forth, for by the word of the Lord were the heavens, and all the hosts, and likewise the earth and the fullness. This goes to reinforce the reason why you must be careful with words, and God's word in your mouth puts you in charge!

In the same vein, many things in life speak, at times, inaudibly. But only few hear. Psalm 19:3, actually declares, **"...no speech nor language, ...their voice is not heard."** The omitted words were not there in the original text, and thus were written in italics in the scripture.

They spoke, and still speak, without words! And may you hear!

So, there are God's handiworks that speak what men should hear so that those who hear may stand-out among others. These handiworks speak about God, His plans and purpose. Again, may you hear their secret messages!

God designed miracles, signs and wonders to speak! They relay God's messages. He ordained it so that those who hear may have faith. While many are carried away with the acts, there is a message hidden therein. No wonder the Lord says signs are for the unbelieving that they may have faith in Him. However, even after signs many still do not believe.

In preparing Moses for his great assignment, God told him -

"And it shall come to pass, if they will not believe thee, neither hearken to the voice of the first sign, that they will believe the voice of the latter sign." –Exodus 4:8.

There are hidden messages or divine voice in the miracles and signs that Moses and Aaron performed in Egypt but the Egyptians, especially Pharaoh, never heard, gave heed nor learned from them and therefore suffered dearly for their chosen deafness!

When the rod of Moses became a serpent and swallowed the serpents of the wise men and sorcerers of Egypt, the voice of the sign was speaking of that which was to come wherein the powers of darkness shall be swallowed up in victory by the irrefutable wisdom and power of the living God!

"And the LORD spake unto Moses and unto Aaron, saying, When Pharaoh shall speak unto you, saying, Shew a miracle for you: then thou shalt say unto Aaron, Take thy rod, and cast it before Pharaoh, and it shall become a serpent. And Moses and Aaron went in unto Pharaoh, and they did so as the LORD had commanded: and Aaron cast down his rod before Pharaoh, and before his servants, and it became a serpent.

Then Pharaoh also called the wise men and the sorcerers: now the magicians of Egypt, they also did in like manner with their enchantments. For they cast down every man his rod, and they

115

became serpents: but Aaron's rod swallowed up their rods."
– Exodus 7:8-12.

This encounter was a foreshadow, a foretelling and a speaking-forth of that which God would do in destroying the powers of the darkness, the prince and the rulers of this dark world for the liberation of the sons of God!

Throughout scriptures, the serpent has always been known for subtleness and sin. And in the plan of salvation, the Messiah will be made sin in order to destroy sin and him who wielded the power of sin. He shall die in order that death may die, He shall be swallowed up in order to swallow the adversary forever! Then it shall come to pass that out of the eater come forth meat! (Judges 14:14)

This is what the miracle and sign was speaking back then, that which is to come to pass in the process of salvation.

Jonah's Big Fish

"But he answered and said unto them, An evil and adulterous generation seeketh after a sign; and there shall no sign be given to it, but the sign of the prophet Jonas." – Matthew 12:39.

Now, let's consider a few scriptures linked together with the sign of the serpent during the Egypt encounter.

In responding to those who were looking for signs from Him in order to believe Him, Jesus informed them that only an adulterous generation would not believe the word of God but would be seeking after signs.

116

However, the sign of Prophet Jonah would be given to them. This implied that what happened to Jonah was a message that points to God's plan of salvation! Jonah's ordeal was not just a coincidence!

"For as Jonas was three days and three nights in the whale's belly; so shall the Son of man be three days and three nights in the heart of the earth." – Matthew 12:40.

This scripture forms part of the process of what the Lord Jesus would go through for the salvation of men. Now, what's really striking with this scripture is the word that the Lord used in describing the **big fish that swallowed Jonah**. He referred to it as **"the whale"**.

Now, in the original story, we were only informed that,

"Now the LORD had prepared a great fish to swallow up Jonah. And Jonah was in the belly of the fish three days and three nights." – Jonah 1:17.

The account in the book of Jonah says God's messenger, Prophet Jonah was swallowed up by **"a great fish"** – Hebrew words **"gadol dag or dawg"**. The word **"gadol"** means great, high or big, and the word **"dag"** implies fish.

However, the Lord Jesus, as a revealer of that which had been hidden from the foundation of the world and the explanation of all things, came and took the matter a little farther than we thought we knew in Prophet Jonah's miracle. Prophet Jonah had played his part in foreshadowing what the Messiah will do in the course of the salvation of mankind.

Now, the Hebrew word translated **"serpent"** in the Exodus account is also one of the words translated as **"sea monster,"** and **"whale"**. It was therefore not coincidental that Jesus our Lord specifically used the word **"whale"** when using Jonah's account to describe what He would go through in the process of salvation.

The serpent, the devil, is the same as the whale Jesus mentioned! Our Lord never shies away from meeting the enemy on his own turf and using his crooked wisdom against him. Remember, Hebrews 2:14 says, *"...that through death he might destroy him that had the power of death, that is, the devil."*

The Sea Serpent & Monster

"And the great dragon was cast out, that old serpent, called the Devil, and Satan, which deceiveth the whole world..."
– Revelation 12:9.

Now, let's consider a little emphasis for us to know at least a little bit of the comprehensiveness of the work of salvation.

"The earth is the LORD'S, and the fulness thereof; the world, and they that dwell therein. For he hath founded it upon the seas, and established it upon the floods." – Psalm 24:1-2.

Psalm 24 makes us to understand that not only is the earth a floating ball, it is floating on a flood or massive body of waters! Therefore, the lower parts of the earth that the Messiah will go before ascending is a place of waters – dark waters! He will first meet the enemy there!

Psalm 18, which is a Messianic prophecy about His contest and deliverance reveals the Messiah was drawn and delivered out of the flood of waters.

"I will call upon the LORD, who is worthy to be praised: so shall I be saved from mine enemies. The sorrows of death compassed me, and the floods of ungodly men made me afraid. The sorrows of hell compassed me about: the snares of death prevented me.

In my distress I called upon the LORD, and cried unto my God: he heard my voice out of his temple, and my cry came before him, even into his ears. The LORD also thundered in the heavens, and the Highest gave his voice; hail stones and coals of fire.

Yea, he sent out his arrows, and scattered them; and he shot out lightnings, and discomfited them. Then the channels of waters were seen, and the foundations of the world were discovered at thy rebuke, O LORD, at the blast of the breath of thy nostrils.

He sent from above, he took me, he drew me out of many waters. He delivered me from my strong enemy, and from them which hated me: for they were too strong for me. They prevented me in the day of my calamity: but the LORD was my stay. He brought me forth also into a large place; he delivered me, because he delighted in me." – Psalm 18:3-6, 13-19.

Now, Jesus had informed us that as Jonah was under the waters in the belly of the whale – a name or word which pointed to the contest in Egypt revealing the enemy as a serpent or sea monster, showed that the battle and war for the souls of mankind, under the earth, was actually in a flood of waters!

119

Whales don't live outside waters. Sea monsters live in deep waters. And if the Messiah was to go into the turf of the adversary, it had to be in the deep waters. And He came out on top by the exceeding greatness of God's mighty power! (Ephesians 1:19-22).

The Brazen Serpent

We need to also touch on this case Jesus mentioned in John 3:14, about the serpent.

"And as Moses lifted up the serpent in the wilderness, even so must the Son of man be lifted up:" - John 3:14.

From here, Jesus the Messiah, like the brazen serpent in the wilderness, will be made sin —as the rod of Aaron became a serpent when dropped on the ground in Egypt. And in coming onto the enemy's turf or ground, being made sin for us, He was going to destroy sin, arrest the arrester and set captives free! What a wisdom beyond anyone's comprehension!

Your enemies are in for a shocker! The Lord shall turn the table against them!

"Or else how can one enter into a strong man's house, and spoil his goods, except he first bind the strong man? and then he will spoil his house." - Matthew 12:29.

Jesus therefore, *"...was made a little lower than the angels for the suffering of death, crowned with glory and honour; that he by the grace of God should taste death for every man. Forasmuch*

120

then as the children are partakers of flesh and blood, he also himself likewise took part of the same; that through death he might destroy him that had the power of death, that is, the devil; " *- Hebrew 2:9, 14.*

The old serpent met his waterloo at the cross! The devil, using death swallowed what was beyond him! And that was his last meal! The resurrected Lord has now abolished death because it touched the untouchable! (2Timothy 1:10). Henceforth, the Lord will make you a bad market for your enemies!

The Lord is going to turn the wisdom of your adversaries to foolishness! Had they known it, they would not have crucified the Lord of glory! Had they known it, they would not have touched you – the apple of God's eye!

"Wherefore he saith, When he ascended up on high, he led captivity captive, and gave gifts unto men. (Now that he ascended, what is it but that he also descended first into the lower parts of the earth? He that descended is the same also that ascended up far above all heavens, that he might fill all things.)" *– Ephesians 4:8-10".*

Before ascending, as signified by the coming out from the waters of Jordan, He first of all went down in His death in order to –

- **Deal with the root of sin**
  "For what the law could not do, in that it was weak through the flesh, God sending his own Son in the likeness of sinful flesh, and for sin, condemned sin in the flesh: That the righteousness of the law might be fulfilled..." *– Romans 8:2-3.*

121

- Reach the captives of sin, the devil and death.
  "For Christ also hath once suffered for sins, the just for the unjust, that he might bring us to God, being put to death in the flesh, but quickened by the Spirit: By which also he went and preached unto the spirits in prison."
  – I Peter 3:18-19.

- Secure forgiveness for believers through His shed blood.
  "And you, being dead in your sins and the uncircumcision of your flesh, hath he quickened together with him, having forgiven you all trespasses." - *Colossians 2:13.*

- Removal of condemnations - Blotting out every handwriting against believers.
  "Blotting out the handwriting of ordinances that was against us, which was contrary to us, and took it out of the way, nailing it to his cross. " - *Colossians 2:14.*

- Secure the total release of captives from captors.
  "And having spoiled principalities and powers, he made a shew of them openly, triumphing over them in it." – *Colossians 2:15.*

- Take preeminence and lead captivity captive
  – arrest the arrester, destroy the destroyer, and having the keys of death and hell, abolish death!
  "Wherefore he saith, When he ascended up on high, he led captivity captive..." – *Ephesians 4:8.*

- Receive gifts of men and for men.
  "Saying with a loud voice, Worthy is the Lamb that was slain to receive power, and riches, and wisdom, and strength, and honour, and glory, and blessing." – *Revelation 5:12.*

"Thou hast ascended on high, thou hast led captivity captive: thou hast received gifts for men; yea, for the rebellious also, that the LORD God might dwell among them." - Psalm 68:18.

"Since thou wast precious in my sight, thou hast been honourable, and I have loved thee: therefore will I give men for thee, and people for thy life."
- Isaiah 43:4

"Therefore being by the right hand of God exalted, and having received of the Father the promise of the Holy Ghost, he hath shed forth this, which ye now see and hear." - Acts 2:33

All these, and far much more, are contained in that which was signified by Christ's baptism at Jordan! When coming out of the waters of Jordan, He was a new man without sin, a man of opened heavens with attestation from the Almighty! What a heritage!

> *"And He brought them to the border of His sanctuary, even to this mountain which His right hand had purchased."*
> *- Psalm 78:54*

Not only are his sins forgiven, the new man comes into an inheritance purchased for him, good works prepared and appointed for him in Christ Jesus! (Ephesians 2:10). Just as Israel came into the land flowing with milk and honey, a land purchased and established by God with His right hand (Exodus 15:17) the new man in Christ is brought into overflowing abundance!

Welcome to overflowing abundance secured by God's right hand man -Jesus Christ!

CHAPTER SIX

The Three Days & Three Nights

*"While it looks like things are out of control,
behind the scenes there is a God who
hasn't surrendered His authority."*

–AW Tozer

Jonah's Three Days and Three Nights

In this discourse of our Redemption Treasures, as part of the steps our Lord took in His redemption process, we need to touch on the period Christ spent in the belly of the earth.

There are tons of immeasurable blessings loaded therein (in the works He accomplished). In order not to over-stretch our scope, we shall simply touch the things that happened within that crucial time space.

> *"And He said unto them, these are the words which I spake unto you, while I was yet with you... Thus it is written, and thus it behoved Christ to suffer, and to rise from the dead the third day."*
> *- Luke 24:44, 46.*

Now, remember that the few seconds a believer is dipped in water at baptism represents the three days and three nights Christ spent in the belly of the earth. And many things, deep things, happened within this space of time.

"For as Jonas was three days and three nights in the whale's belly; so shall the Son of man be three days and three nights in the heart of the earth." – Matthew 12:40.

Time and numbers play very significant roles in spiritual principles, processes and works. As Jonah was prophetically in the belly of the whale for three days and three nights, Jesus was going to be in the heart of the earth in His redemption works for mankind, so that quoted verse says.

Now, why three days and three nights?

There has been so many reasonings, that is arguments, on the exact period Jesus spent in the belly of the earth in His redemption works. However, what we should be concerned more with is the fact that He fulfilled the scriptures, to the very letters. Therefore, whether He actually spent 72 hours or He did His work within the space of the 72 hours, what matters most and should be our focus is that, **He perfected redemption for us during this period of His burial!**

Remember that if Jesus could ask His Father and He would immediately be given twelve legions of angels (Matthew 26:53), then He could have also finished His works under one night, for with God nothing shall be impossible! However, in the things under heavens, time plays a significant role (Ecclesiastes 3:1).

"To every thing there is a season, and a time to every purpose under the heaven." – Ecclesiastes 3:1.

For the period of time Christ spent in the heart of the earth, there is a hidden work the Lord was fulfilling or accomplishing after which tremendous promises are to follow!

Now, there are two things to be brought to mind again in the Lord's Gospel of the Kingdom –

✍ *"...Jesus came into Galilee, preaching the gospel of the kingdom of God, and saying, The time is fulfilled, and the kingdom of God is at hand: repent ye, and believe the gospel." – Mark 1:14-15.*

126

✍ *"And Jesus returned in the power of the Spirit into Galilee... And when he had opened the book, he found the place where it was written, The Spirit of the Lord is upon me, because he hath anointed me to... preach the acceptable year of the Lord ...this day is this scripture fulfilled in your ears."*
- Luke 4:14, 18-19, 21.

In these two scriptures detailing His Gospel after returning from the Jordan water baptism and the wilderness, we see the Lord mentioning the fulfilment of time and making declaration that the **acceptable year of the Lord has come!**

Therefore, having fulfilled the demands of God's law, the promise is no more pending but its time of manifestation has come, already fulfilled!

Now, what you need to understand is that the few seconds you were under water in the course of baptism (representing the three days and three nights Jesus spent in the belly of the earth in His work of salvation) covers a lot of grounds!

When you come to know **what He has fulfilled, which now has become an inheritance for you,** your faith will be ignited to lay hold on them! Remember, your inheritance in Christ is at the mercy of your own faith in Him!

The fulfilled time or times which has now culminated and ushered in the acceptable year of the Lord will be dealt with shortly.

127

The Coverage of Salvation

First, let's touch on the reach or coverage of salvation as a spiritual time and number connect this with the acceptable year of the Lord!

Ours is the God who takes personal responsibility toward His own. As a responsible Creator, the Lord God cares for all (Matthew 6:30). He does not even take delight in the death or the perishing of even the worst of men but that they might be saved and fulfill His purpose (Ezekiel 18:23, 2 Peter 3:9). Therefore, salvation for all men has always been in His heart. However, God has His own designed order of things.

There's no way we can touch on His salvation without mentioning Abraham, God's friend, by and through whom the blessing of salvation for all men was inaugurated. God is the One who picks one and touches the rest! He has all in mind but begins with one!

"As for me, behold, my covenant is with thee, and thou shalt be a father of many nations. Neither shall thy name any more be called Abram, but thy name shall be Abraham; for a father of many nations have I made thee. And I will make thee exceeding fruitful, and I will make nations of thee, and kings shall come out of thee. And I will establish my covenant between me and thee and thy seed after thee in their generations for an everlasting covenant, to be a God unto thee, and to thy seed after thee." – Genesis 17:4-7.

"And in thy seed shall all the nations of the earth be blessed; because thou hast obeyed my voice."- Genesis 22:18.

Then through that one man, upon whom God puts His hand, He begins to expand the plan to cover all men!

Your family, village, town, nation is in God's mind. He is starting with you, yes you! There's a greater work He shall accomplish in and through you!

As we do not wish to drift too much away from the scope of this book, we are merely touching the expounded order by which salvation, in God's plan, covered all men.

Jesus Christ became that seed promised to Abraham, the promised seed that will bruise the head of Satan (destroy or end his rule or administration) and will also possess the gates of His enemies (Genesis 3:15, Genesis 22:17). And by His circumcision in the flesh, Jesus triggered the Abrahamic covenant with God by which all men would be brought into God's living relationship and rule. (Colossians 2:11). Remember, He stepped into humanity as the Son of Man.

Now, God's salvation through Jesus Christ is a comprehensive work that, according to the Abrahamic promise, includes the Gentile nations, and not just for the Jews only. His salvation was destined unto the uttermost part of the earth. And there is that which represent the Gentiles in God's programme. Numerous scriptures, prophetically and directly, informs and affirms that He shall reign over all nations!

"And he said, It is a light thing that thou shouldest be my servant to raise up the tribes of Jacob, and to restore the preserved of Israel: I will also give thee for a light to the Gentiles, that thou mayest be my salvation unto the end of the earth." - Isaiah 49:6.

Counting the three days and three nights in the terms of hours, we see that it amounts to 72 hours in the heart of the earth in the work of salvation. And, I strongly believe, this is where the salvation works for all men, including the Gentile nations, come in together with the fulfilment of times prophesied and promised of old.

Throughout scriptures, we see the number seven and seventy playing significant roles of representing time for administration over nations, and the multiples of seven representing atonement of sin, and subsequent freedom. These are the times gathered up together in Christ Jesus!

Now, lets' look at some scriptures directly regarding this, and we begin with an unusual scripture:

"Remember the days of old, consider the years of many generations: ask thy father, and he will shew thee; thy elders, and they will tell thee. When the most High divided to the nations their inheritance, when he separated the sons of Adam, he set the bounds of the people according to the number of the children of Israel. For the LORD'S portion is his people; Jacob is the lot of his inheritance." - Deuteronomy 32:7-9.

From this scripture, when God was allotting inheritance or lands to the nations, few things happened:

-   Firstly, He divided to the nations their inheritance
-   Secondly, their administration will be according to the number of the children of Israel.
-   Thirdly, He took personal charge over the nation of the children of Israel

130

"The Most High assigned nations their lands; he determined where peoples should live. He assigned to each nation a heavenly being, but Jacob's descendants he chose for himself." – Deut. 32:8-9 (GNB -Good News Bible)

God chose the children of Israel, referred to as Jacob, unto Himself as His portion and inheritance, as He divided to the nations their inheritance, and set their bounds or will administer them according to the number of the children of Israel. God had something in view – ruling the nations through His children! Now, what is this number?

All Bible scholars agree that this number is seventy – the number that identifies greatly with Jacob in all his life history. In a way, Israel through Jacob's life became God's measuring line in this case, so to speak!

"All the souls that came with Jacob into Egypt, which came out of his loins, besides Jacob's sons' wives, all the souls were threescore and six; And the sons of Joseph, which were born him in Egypt, were two souls: all the souls of the house of Jacob, which came into Egypt, were threescore and ten." – Genesis 46:26-27.

Now, the laws governing sevens or multiples of seven were very evident in the life of Jacob. It could be the reason why his name was mentioned in the scripture of Deuteronomy 32:9. Assuredly Jacob's mention was not a casual or coincidental thing. The nation of Israel could have been referred to as the seed or children of Abraham, but the scripture zeroed in on Jacob as the Lord's inheritance.

It would be noted that Jacob served for his wives seven years twice, and the next six years served for his cattle or increase.

131

At the next seventh year, he got "liberated" from the tyranny of Laban. In all, he served under Laban for twenty years (Genesis 31:41).

Also, when Jacob passed on, he was mourned in Egypt for seventy days (Genesis 50:3). Also, Jacob lived for one hundred and forty-seven years (147 years) which if counted in seven Sabbath years comes to three (that is 49 years three times). All these things have meaning which Christ came to fulfill!

The Seventy Elders of Israel

We are coming to how the Gentiles are linked up in the course of salvation which God had promised will reach unto the ends of earth.

Now, in the course of his administration over the children of Israel, Moses was instructed to select seventy men who would bear the burden with him. Upon these men God took of the spirit that was upon Moses and gave to them. These men stood in Moses' office to help judge Israel.

"And the LORD said unto Moses, Gather unto me seventy men of the elders of Israel, whom thou knowest to be the elders of the people, and officers over them; and bring them unto the tabernacle of the congregation, that they may stand there with thee. And I will come down and talk with thee there: and I will take of the spirit which is upon thee, and will put it upon them; and they shall bear the burden of the people with thee, that thou bear it not thyself alone." – Numbers 11:6-7.

This event and number must be prophetic as Jesus toiled the same line in His earthly ministry. So when Jesus came, He first appointed twelve men (the number of the tribes of Israel) whom He named Apostles. These are the ones chosen from among the multitudes that would be with Him and whom He may send forth to preach (Mark 3:14).

When these **twelve disciples,** prophetically representing the twelve tribes of Israel, were first sent forth to preach, they were **not to go to the Gentiles but preach only to the house of Israel.** Their given instructions were very clear.

"These twelve Jesus sent forth, and commanded them, saying, Go not into the way of the Gentiles, and into any city of the Samaritans enter ye not: But go rather to the lost sheep of the house of Israel." – Matthew 10:5-6.

Here's the Messiah of the whole world ministering only to Israelites. **Didn't He come to die for the sin of the whole world?** What about others who are not Israelites? But Jesus didn't forget His assignment! It's just that everything must be done decently and in order. Even in God's programme for the nations, He starts with Israel.

According to Isaiah 49:6, *"He will raise up the tribes of Jacob and restore the preserved of Israel..."*

There's an account in scriptures about a Canaanite woman who came to Jesus and persistently begged for her daughter to be healed. Even though the Lord did not answer her, His eventual response was puzzling as He answered, that **He was sent only to the lost sheep of the house of Israel.**

But thank God for this woman's faith that made the Lord to release her miracle to her!

"Then Jesus went thence, and departed into the coasts of Tyre and Sidon. And, behold, a woman of Canaan came out of the same coasts, and cried unto him, saying, Have mercy on me, O Lord, thou Son of David; my daughter is grievously vexed with a devil. But he answered her not a word. And his disciples came and besought him, saying, Send her away; for she crieth after us.

But he answered and said, I am not sent but unto the lost sheep of the house of Israel. Then came she and worshipped him, saying, Lord, help me.

But he answered and said, It is not meet to take the children's bread, and to cast it to dogs. And she said, Truth, Lord: yet the dogs eat of the crumbs which fall from their masters' table. Then Jesus answered and said unto her, O woman, great is thy faith: be it unto thee even as thou wilt. And her daughter was made whole from that very hour." – Matthew 15:21-28.

Don't give up beloved, you are in God's agenda! He has something in store that you can access! This woman's persistent faith changed the game. Even though it was not her turn for a miracle, yet she would not take no for an answer nor be offended by the statement that seemed derogatory. She focused on her miracle, and got it! Your faith in the Lord's goodness and mercy shall not be denied!

"After these things the Lord appointed other seventy also, and sent them two and two before his face into every city and place, whither he himself would come." – Luke 10:1.

Then Jesus appointed **other seventy** also who would go into EVERY city and place He was going to come (prophetically unto the ends of the earth, the Gentile nations). The Lord had initially restricted Himself to the Jews, but now He is going to other nations.

These disciples and their number represent the Lord's administration over every other place that the first twelve disciples did not cover in their first assignment. By this instruction, the Gentiles and Samaritans are finally brought into the plan of salvation. The "seventy" represent all believers, under the Lord's command, who will go all over the world, in His authority and anointing, to preach the Gospel to all creatures!

This is the number of the children of Israel, spiritual Israel – the believers in Christ Jesus, foretold in Deuteronomy 32:8-9.

When Jesus rose from the dead He commanded: *"Go ye into all the world..."* (Mark 16:15) because all authority over all the nations is now in His hand, and He therefore sends forth His disciples to them!

The Sanhedrin

"And the LORD said unto Moses, Gather unto me seventy men of the elders of Israel, whom thou knowest to be the elders of the people, and officers over them; and bring them unto the tabernacle of the congregation, that they may stand there with thee."- Numbers 11:16.

In the mirror of the appointed seventy elders of Moses –who were to be judges over the whole Israel on his behalf, the members of the Sanhedrin, the religious body that governs the children of Israel were seventy in number. This group of elders of Israel saw deep into the systematic appointments of the Lord, the twelve and the seventy, and felt threatened that if care was not taken they would be replaced!

They, therefore, we were the ones who plotted to kill and destroy Jesus. They colluded with Judas – the betrayer, arrested and bound Jesus, and handed Him over to the Gentiles to be killed.

"Then gathered the chief priests and the Pharisees a council, and said, What do we? for this man doeth many miracles. If we let him thus alone, all men will believe on him: and the Romans shall come and take away both our place and nation... Then from that day forth they took counsel together for to put him to death." – John 11:47-48, 53.

Fearing that they would lose their place, they put Jesus to death, which Apostle Peter spoke to their face!

"Then Peter, being full of the Holy Spirit, said to them, O you rulers of the people and men of authority, If we are questioned today about a good work done to a man who was ill, as to how he has been made well, Take note, all of you, and all the people of Israel, that in the name of Jesus Christ of Nazareth, whom you put to death on the cross, whom God gave back from the dead, even through him is this man now before you completely well. He is the stone which you builders had no use for, but which has been made the chief stone of the building." – Acts 4:8-11.

The Fulfillment of Time & Times

"Having made known unto us the mystery of his will, according to his good pleasure which he hath purposed in himself: That in the dispensation of the fulness of times he might gather together in one all things in Christ, both which are in heaven, and which are on earth; even in him." – Ephesians 1:9-10.

All times and the prophecies or promises associated with them all got headed up in Christ Jesus. In Him and through Him, all things were brought together and personified in His person. After His sacrifice, time and space came into His power. This is one of the reasons He declared that: *"...The Son of man is Lord also of the sabbath." – Mark 2:28.*

Now, what is the time or times which Jesus fulfilled when He spent three days and three nights in the heart of the earth?

I believe so strongly that because seventy is within the space of the seventy-two hours, comprising the three days and three nights, that His salvation unto the ends of the earth - involving all the Gentile nations, was fulfilled and perfected! The atonement for the transgressions of all nations was carried out within that time space!

Remember, He is the Lamb of God who took away the sin of the whole world, not just of Israel. Under Judaism, the Passover lamb, sacrifice and atonement was just for the Jews and proselytes. However, God's Passover Lamb and sacrifice is for all nations.

Remember also that when Jesus rose from the dead, He declared that ALL authority in heaven and on earth has been given unto Him! He is Lord over all the nations! And He declared that His disciples should go therefore into all nations and to all creatures and preach the Gospel! It's because He has reconciled all things unto Himself through the blood of His cross.

Two scriptures succinctly touch on the Lord Jesus Christ covering all things in His work of redemption for it pleased the Father that in Him all fullness – of things in heaven and on earth, should dwell!

- *"For it pleased the Father that in him should all fullness dwell; And, having made peace through the blood of his cross, by him to reconcile all things unto himself; by him, I say, whether they be things in earth, or things in heaven." – Colossians 1:19-20*

- *"(Now that he ascended, what is it but that he also descended first into the lower parts of the earth? He that descended is the same also that ascended up far above all heavens, that he might fill all things.)" – Ephesians 4:9-10*

Multiples of Sevens

Within the space of the seventy-two hours in the belly of the earth, let's consider a few multiples of sevens that involves sins and atonements which He fulfilled.

✍ The Lord's Release

"At the end of every seven years thou shalt make a

release. And this is the manner of the release: Every creditor that lendeth ought unto his neighbour shall release it; he shall not exact it of his neighbour, or of his brother; because it is called the LORD'S release. Of a foreigner thou mayest exact it again: but that which is thine with thy brother thine hand shall release." – Deuteronomy 15:1-3

This is why Jesus preached the Gospel to the poor (or afflicted). For, having paid the price, they have now been released from every manner of debt (or affliction).

✍ **The Land Sabbaths**

"And the LORD spake unto Moses in mount Sinai, saying, Speak unto the children of Israel, and say unto them, When ye come into the land which I give you, then shall the land keep a sabbath unto the LORD. Six years thou shalt sow thy field, and six years thou shalt prune thy vineyard, and gather in the fruit thereof; But in the seventh year shall be a sabbath of rest unto the land, a sabbath for the LORD: thou shalt neither sow thy field, nor prune thy vineyard." – Leviticus 25:1-4

When Israel was exiled to Babylon, they were to remain there for seventy years in order that the land may enjoy its Sabbaths. Their disobedience in not observing the land's Sabbath led to their captivity and this sin was going to take seventy years to be atoned for.

"For thus saith the LORD, That after seventy years be accomplished at Babylon I will visit you, and perform my good word toward you, in causing you to return to this place. For I know the thoughts that I think toward you, saith the LORD, thoughts of peace, and not of evil, to give you an expected end. Then shall ye call upon me, and ye shall go and pray unto me, and I will hearken unto you..." – Jeremiah 29:10-14.

"And them that had escaped from the sword carried he away to Babylon; where they were servants to him and his sons until the reign of the kingdom of Persia: To fulfil the word of the LORD by the mouth of Jeremiah, until the land had enjoyed her sabbaths: for as long as she lay desolate she kept sabbath, to fulfil threescore and ten years." – 2 Chronicles 36:20-21.

So there's a Sabbath rest unto the land which Israel was to observe and during this rest, the Lord will supernaturally make provisions available for His children.

The Lord's Jubilee

"And thou shalt number seven sabbaths of years unto thee, seven times seven years; and the space of the seven sabbaths of years shall be unto thee forty and nine years. Then shalt thou cause the trumpet of the jubilee to sound on the tenth day of the seventh month, in the day of atonement shall ye make the trumpet sound throughout all your land.

And ye shall hallow the fiftieth year, and proclaim

liberty throughout all the land unto all the inhabitants thereof: it shall be a jubilee unto you; and ye shall return every man unto his possession, and ye shall return every man unto his family.

A jubilee shall that fiftieth year be unto you: ye shall not sow, neither reap that which groweth of itself in it, nor gather the grapes in it of thy vine undressed. For it is the jubilee; it shall be holy unto you: ye shall eat the increase thereof out of the field. In the year of this jubilee ye shall return every man unto his possession."
– Leviticus 25:8-13.

Yes, jubilee has to do with the fiftieth year but its declaration is from the forty-ninth year after seven times seven Sabbaths has been counted. It is the year God promised abundance for His people because during the Jubilee year, they would neither sow nor reap.

In the same vein, we are not blessed in Christ because of our works or efforts but because the blessings are already laid up in Him! We are brought into abundance! (Ephesians 1:3, Philippians 4:19)

✍ Seventy Times Seven

Our Lord was once asked how many times a brother should offend before he should or can be forgiven.

Now, the numbers mentioned in the conversation were not coincidental. There was the idea that atonement for transgressions carried the seven

141

period, and so Peter asked if it was seven times. However, Jesus replied that it was until seventy times seven.

"Then came Peter to him, and said, Lord, how oft shall my brother sin against me, and I forgive him? **till seven times?** *Jesus saith unto him, I say not unto thee, Until seven times: but, **Until seventy times seven.**"* – Matthew 18:21-22.

This declared number of figure had to do with the atoning work of the Messiah in outing an end to sin, achieve forgiveness and release for all and bring in righteousness.

✍ **Daniel's Seventy Weeks**

"At the beginning of thy supplications the commandment came forth, and I am come to shew thee; for thou art greatly beloved: therefore understand the matter, and consider the vision. Seventy weeks are determined upon thy people and upon thy holy city, to finish the transgression, and to make an end of sins, and to make reconciliation for iniquity, and to bring in everlasting righteousness, and to seal up the vision and prophecy, and to anoint the most Holy." – Daniel 9:23-24.

This singular scripture seem to have packed so much promises and prophecies that the Prince, the Messiah was going to fulfill altogether! These are the things fully fulfilled by Christ in the course of the seventy-two hours spanning the three days and three nights in the heart of the earth!

142

In the course of this period of time, He:

- **Paid the price and penalty to finish all transgressions** (Isaiah 53:5, I Peter 3:18)
- **He made an end to sin** (Isaiah 53:10, Romans 8:3, 2 Cor. 5:21, I Peter 2:24)
- **He made reconciliation for iniquity** (Isaiah 53:6, Colossians 1:20, I Peter 2:25)
- **He brought in everlasting righteousness** (Isaiah 53:11, Romans 10:4, Romans 5:19, 2 Cor. 5:21)
- **He confirmed the visions and prophecies regarding atonement for sins** (Luke 24:27, 44)
- **Ushered in the coming in of the anointing of the Holy Spirit** (Luke 24:49, Acts 2:32-33)

Please, recall that when Jesus was coming out from the water in Jordan, the Holy Spirit came, lightened upon Him and therefore Jesus of Nazareth became anointed of God! He therefore declared, *"The Spirit of the Lord is upon Me because He hath anointed Me..."* – Luke 4:19. That is the manifestation of God's Holy One which Daniel 9:24 speaks about.

Recall also, that when Christ was raised from the dead, in the fulfilment of the coming out from the waters, He was declared to be the Son of God according to the Spirit of Holiness!

"Concerning his Son Jesus Christ our Lord, which was made of the seed of David according to the flesh; And declared to be the Son of God with power, according to the spirit of holiness, by the resurrection from the dead." – *Romans 1:3-4.*

143

From these highlighted points, the Lord's accomplishments within the three days and three nights in the grave are now very clear. To the disciples, His time in the grave was the longest time they ever knew as all their hope seemed dashed away at His death. But the Lord was not idle about their case. In fact, He was accomplishing the greatest work for all creation! Eternity was involved.

When He rose, and revealed Himself to them as promised, their joy knew no limit! The same set of people who were afraid of others and often locked the door against themselves, after Pentecost, became so bold and declared the Lordship of Jesus without trembling before any man.

The Pentecost was the fulfilment of the "anoint a Holy" portion of Daniel 9:24, in which the Holy Ghost –the Promise Jesus received from the Father and therefore shed forth upon those who believe and receive Him!

Welcome to His new life under the government of His Holy Spirit!

CHAPTER SEVEN

The Price & the Prize

*"He looks neither at the aggregate of fat
nor at the number of burnt offerings
but solely at the sum of obedience to Him."*

–Watchman Nee

Paying The Price and the Prize

"Having predestinated us unto the adoption of children by Jesus Christ to himself, according to the good pleasure of his will, to the praise of the glory of his grace, wherein he hath made us accepted in the beloved. In whom we have redemption through his blood, the forgiveness of sins, according to the riches of his grace."
– Ephesians 1:5-7.

"Remember that He who rose from the dead, rose to pour out His Holy Spirit into human lives, and by that Spirit, to make available to any individual all the fulness of Himself, twenty-four hours a day."
- Ray C. Stedman

Scriptures, according to the prophecies of the law, inform us that the life of the flesh is in the blood and God has given the blood to make atonement for our souls (Leviticus 17:11).

We therefore need to briefly revisit a more detailed process or works of redemption in the fulfilment of Daniel 9:24, which foretold the Messiah paying the penalty for sin, iniquities, transgressions, the ushering in of everlasting righteousness and the release of the anointing.

Dealing with All Dirt

"Thus shall ye separate the children of Israel from their uncleanness; that they die not in their uncleanness, when they defile my tabernacle that is among them." *- Leviticus 15:31.*

146

In the law, there are processes of dealing with uncleanness or impurities before the unclean person is brought back into fellowship. We have the processes iterated in Leviticus chapters 14 and 15, for all manner of uncleanness such as that of a leper or leprous house, discharge from a man, a woman's periodic discharge, just to mention a few.

It will be noted that people with uncleanness are often isolated or shut out of the public just as sin shuts a man out of God's reach and presence (Isaiah 59:1-2). It was to keep such from polluting others by their uncleanness. After some period of time, they will be examined by the priests, and if deemed fit to return into fellowship, sacrifices will be made and the blood of the sacrifices shall be sprinkled on the altar and upon the victim of uncleanness. After this atonement, anointing oil will be applied on such a person before final readmission.

In some cases, for example, a leper will wash himself, shave off his hair, get sanctified by the blood of sacrifice and afterward anointed with oil before being readmitted into the Camp. This process may take several days.

Now, these are types and shadows of the things Christ has fulfilled in Himself for us! By His shed blood, He made perfect atonement for mankind, purged us from all sin and thereafter qualified us to be anointed with the Holy Spirit.

However, our emphasis this for this time is on the shed blood of redemption. As our High Priest, He had us in mind, carried us in His heart when He willingly gave Himself for sacrifice and endured the whole process (Hebrews 12:2). The new creation, with you as part of it, was the object in view!

You see, there are eight times or places where Christ Jesus shed His blood as part of His entire work of redemption for humanity. When we have some understanding of this, it will help in fortifying our faith and we shall be able to withstand any assault of the enemy and overcome his lies.

The first of the times Jesus Christ shed His blood was to bring us into covenant relationship with God while the other seven times were in the process of He going to the cross. You will recall that **"Eight"** is the number of newness while **"Seven"** is the spiritual number of perfection, fullness, wholeness or completeness.

Remember also, that the shedding of blood cancels out sin and opens a new door for change from one state or place to a better one. Wherever then you see the blood of Christ shed for you, in His process of redemption, see the door of breakthrough and deliverance it has opened and take it! (Hebrews 10:20).

In summary, the total number of times He shed His precious blood brought us into the new creation order (2Cor. 5:17) of His Father. Now, His blood shedding processes are:

1.   The Circumcision of Christ

"In whom also ye are circumcised with the circumcision made without hands, in putting off the body of the sins of the flesh by the circumcision of Christ."– Colossians 2:11.

This is first and foremost! It is the foundation for other works of redemption. According to God's covenant order

148

with Abraham, **every male child born into his house must be circumcised in the foreskin of his flesh on the eight day** (Genesis 17:10-14). There is a foreshadowing in this ordinance – the separation of the flesh from the spirit.

The Lord's process of redemption began with His circumcision by which His death (putting off the body of sins of the flesh) was foretold. By this process, atonement and deliverance from the power of the sinful flesh was established.

As the number eight spiritually speaking refers to a new beginning, His circumcision points to man's new relationship and walk with God. Redemption works began here in His flesh.

As a Jew, this shedding of His blood was to bring everyone in Him into the Abrahamic covenant (Galatians 3:14). His circumcision therefore opened the door for every believer and receiver of His Lordship to receive the promise of the Spirit. It made way for every believer to have access to all the Abrahamic blessings (Luke 1:68-75). Yours is therefore truly an enviable heritage!

"For he is not a Jew, which is one outwardly; neither is that circumcision, which is outward in the flesh: But he is a Jew, which is one inwardly; and circumcision is that of the heart, in the spirit, and not in the letter; whose praise is not of men, but of God." – Romans 2:28-29.

Remember, God's intervention in Egypt for the release of Israel was not because the children of Israel had any covenant with God but because God would fulfill His promise to Abraham and his seed after him (Exodus 3:23-25).

And history informs us of what God did for the release of His people. So shall heaven fight for you too! By the faithfulness of the covenant keeping God, whoever or whatsoever won't let you go but hold you captive shall go for you!

"And if ye be Christ's, then are ye Abraham's seed, and heirs according to the promise." – Galatians 3:29.

God's covenant blessing to Abraham also included his seed after him! (Genesis 22:17-18). By this, it is hoped you can now see a world of promises awaiting you! Abraham's blessings will not just be songs to you henceforth, but promises that shall find practical fulfilment in your very life!

2. Garden of Gethsemane & Hair Pulling

"I gave... my cheeks to them that plucked off the hair: I hid not my face from shame and spitting." – Isaiah 50:6.

There are two places where blood was shed from the face of Jesus Christ for us. The first was when He was praying in the garden of Gethsemane and had to submit to the will of God.

It was a time of great agony as there was tremendous battle He was fighting in the spirit.

"And being in an agony he prayed more earnestly: and his sweat was as it were great drops of blood falling down to the ground." – Luke 22:44.

By His shed blood here, He opened the way for the will of God, as it is done in heaven, to be done on earth and in our lives. In the garden, He submitted totally to the Father's will. He settled our case through His blood here!

"Jesus [Christ] didn't sweat in the wilderness but in the garden [of Gethsemane, the place of the press] when [God's] redemption [promise] was closest for us! - Luke 22:44. [Look away and] See beyond the [present, immense] pressures, you're nearer the promises [of redemption, breakthroughs, more] than ever! -Hebrews 12:2"
- Saheed Ogunsola

Henceforth, according to His will and word, your days shall be as the days of heaven on earth! Whatever heaven provides, as God's will, shall never be missing in your earthly affairs again! By His blood, you can bring the will of God to come to pass in your life, here and now!

The second shedding of blood from Christ's face was when He was blindfolded, smitten or struck on the face severally and His beard was plucked off by His mockers.

"And the men that held Jesus mocked him, and smote him. And when they had blindfolded him, they struck him on the face, and asked him, saying, Prophesy, who is it that smote thee?"
– Luke 22:63-64.

As they smote the Lord relentlessly, they also plucked off His beard. The Hebrew word used in Isaiah 50:6, means properly to polish, to sharpen or make smooth. The Orientals hold beards in great veneration and take them as marks of honour.

151

It is one of the most terrible indignities, infamous and humiliating for man's beards to be shaved off, plucked off, as they did to Christ.

The Lord never hid His face from the shame so that you and I may never know shame or reproach again! His shed blood here therefore shall give you beauty for ashes! Your mockers shall never have the final laugh!

"... I hid not my face from shame and spitting." – Isaiah 50:6.

It was never recorded that these acts of the soldiers were normal as none of these acts were meted out to the two thieves crucified alongside Jesus. His case was uncommon just to make your life peculiar!

Not only did they relentlessly slap Him and pulled off Christ's beard but they spat on Him! Now, to spit on anyone, among the Orientals and even in the law, is regarded as an expression of the highest insult, indignity and degrading. Yet He opened not His mouth!

Now His result, through the shedding of His blood and humiliation, has cancelled out any and every insult the enemy may want to heap upon your life! He has now called you unto glory and virtue not shame and reproach! (2 Peter 1:4).

Christ's face, marred beyond recognition before His death was never the same after He was raised from the dead. Even Apostle John the Beloved could not look into this same face that had been transformed! When John saw Him, he fell before Christ as one dead! (Revelation 1:14, 17).

152

By His blood, you have the right to stand on this covenant ground to receive grace to beautify your life! It's yours to receive!

3.   Scourging of Pilate and the Soldiers

"I gave my back to the smiters, and my cheeks to them that plucked off the hair..." – Isaiah 50:6.

The terrible whips given to Jesus on His back, for no crime He committed, brought the shedding of blood through the stripes thereon. Not only does this make atonement for our healing and health but also that we may not be without divine backing.

"When Pilate saw that he could prevail nothing... Then released he Barabbas unto them: and when he had scourged Jesus, he delivered him to be crucified." – Matthew 27:24-26.

The law recommends not more than forty stripes or strokes (Deuteronomy 25:3) but we are not told the Romans regarded that. The Man of Galilee was beaten mercilessly! However, the punishment that secured our peace was laid on Him and the resulting stripes guaranteed divine health and healing for us!

Having made this atonement for you, no disease therefore should survive in your body! The penalty has been paid, and the payment is still valid!

Also, the back signifies the part of our body not covered by the armour but He shed His blood there that we might be fortified all around!

4.   The Crown of Thorns

"Then released he Barabbas unto them: and when he had scourged Jesus, he delivered him to be crucified. Then the soldiers of the governor took Jesus into the common hall, and gathered unto him the whole band of soldiers. And they stripped him, and put on him a scarlet robe. And when they had platted a crown of thorns, they put it upon his head, and a reed in his right hand: and they bowed the knee before him, and mocked him, saying, Hail, King of the Jews!" - Matthew 27:26-29.

When they platted on Him the crown of thorns, the mockers were unaware of what they were doing! So too shall your adversaries forever remain in error and help you fulfill God's will for your life!

As important as every part of the body may be, the head stands out! This is the capital, the seat of the government of a man's life! The head is the controlling centre, as everything is linked up with the head (Colossians 2:19). Once anything goes wrong with the head, the whole body pays for it! Whatever takes control at the head, controls every part of the body! Jesus came to take that control back through His atoning blood!

The future lies with the head as it houses the faculties of vision, reasoning, and controls every part of the body.

"And you, that were sometime alienated and enemies in your mind by wicked works, yet now hath he reconciled."
– Colossians 1:21.

The sin of Adam brought about the darkening of the mind and understanding of man right from the beginning, and by this, all his works are polluted before God! (Ephesians 4:17-18)

Remember, because of sin and the influence of devil over man's life, the imagination of man's heart had been evil continually, and this brought judgement (Genesis 6:5). The heart of man is deceitful above all things and desperately wicked, and even no man, but God, can know it! (Jeremiah 17:9).

> *"For from within, out of the heart of men, proceed evil thoughts, adulteries, fornications, murders, thefts ... foolishness: all these evil things come from within and defile the man."*
> -*Mark 7:21-23*

This is why Jesus never committed himself to any man for He knew what was in man (John 2:24-25). Man had been alienated, separated from God through his thoughts, out of which proceeded all his abominable works (Matthew 15:18-19, Mark 7:21).

The crown of thorns brought the shedding of blood from Christ's head, and therefore made atonement for the sins of the head and mind. His blood came to open the veil spread over all men, and thereby destroy the death sentence upon man! (Isaiah 25:7-8)

Also, the curse and the devil's government over man became broken and ended by this atonement (Genesis 3:17-19).

You will see that wherever Jesus stepped into, the earth yielded its increase unto Him (Psalm 65:9-13), abundance

155

followed Him. The river of His life made everything to bud, grow and bring forth fruits. He was excused from the curse of the first Adam. And this is your lot, through Him, this day forward!

Part of the curse on the serpent was that dust will be its meat (Genesis 3:14). Now, there is a link with Adam here as in the curse placed over him, he would return to dust for he was made from dust (Genesis 3:19). This implies he was going to become the serpent's meat! This is why the devil afflicts men with all manner of bodily diseases.

By the atoning blood of Jesus Christ, that curse is lifted off you! You shall no more become the serpent's meat! Diseases shall no more ravage your body, by the power of the great Physician!

The earth shall yield its increase unto you as your desert shall become a fruitful field! The promise is waiting for you to take possession of it! (Isaiah 28:17, Isaiah 51:3). Whatever Jesus held in His hands prospered, so shall it be for you also! Having opened a way through His blood for you unto prosperity, you shall therefore never be stranded in life again!

The evil veil that has kept you from God's abundant provision for your life is destroyed by His blood today! No more shall lack be your lot! (Isaiah 26:6-8). Blindness of heart, mind and eyes becomes history through his blood from today forward! (John 8:12). All you have missed shall He open your eyes to see and begin to possess!

As Christ becomes your head, endless increase becomes your lot today forward! (Isaiah 9:7, ICor. 11:3). As your head and

Lord, whatever can't be above Him, subdue Him or lord it over Him, shall not have dominion over you again!

God's promises are waiting for you, and they can't be yours until you appropriate the blood to take possession of them! (Isaiah 28:17, Isaiah 51:3). Open your mouth therefore and begin to possess your possessions by the blood of the Lamb! Having opened a way through His blood for you unto prosperity, you shall therefore never be stranded in life again!

5.   Crushed under the Weight of the Cross

"And the government shall be upon His shoulders..."
– Isaiah 9:7.

The weight of the cross was such that it brought bruises on his shoulders. This blood shed here is about the weight of sin that destroyed humanity. By this He broke the curse of the weight of sin and the burdens of life for us. Now, His rest is your lot!

"Come to me all ye that are weary and heavy laden, and I will give you rest..." – Matthew 11:28.

Also, the government of our lives is now upon His shoulders. And Isaiah prophesied endless increases under His government (Isaiah 9:7).

By His blood, where others cannot reach or where men thought you could never reach, you shall surpass! The burden Bearer, yoke Destroyer and great Helper shall not abandon you!

6. The Nailing of His Hands

"...They pierced my hands and my feet." - Psalm 22:16.

By the nailing on the cross, Christ shed His blood through His hands to atone for, free and deliver us from the repercussions of the wicked works man has ever committed. Every wicked deed by man was thus laid upon Him!

Throughout scripture and in life generally, **the hand is the most frequently symbolized part of the body**. It signifies human actions, work, power, strength, rulership, dominion etc. By the original sin, every work of man has been contrary to God (Colossians 1:21).

In order **to make our works acceptable unto God, atonement is a must!** By the sanctification through His blood, may your work henceforth find acceptance before God!

The Hebrew root word translated as **"piercing"** in Psalm 22:16, implies to **"dig"**. Though scholars argue over the use of the word translated **"pierce"**. Nevertheless there's no doubt holes were bored through the hands of Jesus Christ on the cross (John 20:25).

By this atonement, nothing good leaks out of your hands again! No good thing drops off your hands or fail again! Whatever you lay your hand upon shall prosper! By His shed blood here, all connections with hands shall work for you!

7. The Nailing of His feet

"...They pierced my hands and my feet." - Psalm 22:16.

His feet were pierced with nails as they were fastened to His cross, and the shed blood here was to make atonement for things pertaining to man's feet.

The feet of man had taken him away from God and strayed from the path of righteousness. Man had entered into wrong things and places through sin, and the end of such is death (Proverbs 14:12, Proverbs 21:15).

Every step in rebellion had thus been atoned for by the shedding of Christ's blood. You shall not miss the way of peace again! As you walk in and through life, your feet shall not slip!

By the blood of His cross, your steps shall be washed with butter (Deut. 33:24, Job 29:6). By His blood, we now walk in the light of life and dominion over all the works of the devil!

"All we like sheep have gone astray; we have turned every one to his own way; and the LORD hath laid on him the iniquity of us all." - Isaiah 53:6.

How else shall we walk with the Lord if atonement is not made in this area? How shall we stand before Him or on His holy ground? The blood made a way for us! Henceforth, you shall not stray from His presence!

Feet represent how far we shall go in life. And when He said *"go ye into all the world,"* it was because He has completed His work in that area that wherever the soles of your feet shall thread, at His command, it shall be yours for dominion!

Everywhere Jesus Himself walked, as promised to Israel, it was in dominion. Henceforth, you shall not stray from the path of life! Your feet shall be washed with butter, and you shall dip your feet in oil! No devil shall be able to withstand you all the days of your life!

8. Piercing on the side

"Then came the soldiers, and brake the legs of the first, and of the other which was crucified with him. But when they came to Jesus, and saw that he was dead already, they brake not his legs: But one of the soldiers with a spear pierced his side, and forthwith came there out blood and water." – John 19:32-34.

Having been found to have given up the ghost, committing His Spirit unto the Father, His side was pierced with a spear and water and blood gushed out. His heart was ruptured for our sins. He suffered broken heart that ours may be made whole.

Our willful sins, for out of the heart proceeds evils and defilements (Mark 7:21), were also atoned for in this part of His body. Remember, the scripture that **the heart of man is deceitful above all things and desperately wicked** (Jeremiah 17:9).

Also, side is a type of companionship, relationship and fellowship. Jesus atoned for every failed relationship of man here, every failure of man with man and every failure of man with God!

Also, Genesis 2:21-22, informs us that Eve, the first woman, was made from the side of man. You shall never lack true companionship all your days again! Remember, God promised never to leave nor forsake (Hebrews 13:5). Unbroken fellowship and companionship got guaranteed by His atonement here!

In summary, we thus see that through the shedding of His blood, Jesus made a full atonement for all our sins, known and unknown, iniquities and transgressions, He brought in righteousness and sanctified us through His blood to make us ready for the anointing of the Holy Ghost to fulfill the law and the prophecies in Daniel 9:24 and Isaiah 53.

The Holy Ghost and the Prize!

"For, behold, I create new heavens and a new earth: and the former shall not be remembered, nor come into mind. And it shall come to pass, that before they call, I will answer; and while they are yet speaking, I will hear." – Isaiah 65:17, 24.

In the new creation order, we are to live in answers! As written in this scripture, things are radically different from the former wherein man sweats to eat, and even the earth would yield thorns and thistles.

161

But because of what the Redeemer has secured through His perfect sacrifice, before a request is made, answers are already waiting! And this is what Christ has accomplished and opened up for every believer in and with this new life! **You are to live provision minded and not need minded!** Now, Philippians 4:19, should make a better sense that supply is the next deal because provision is already available!

In this new life, even as Jesus said you could ask Him or the Father for anything, and it shall be done (John 14:13-14, John 15:7, John 16:23). His Name has thus become the greatest password to open the greatest treasure for every need!

There is nothing you could ever ask that is beyond the provision of His grace! (Jeremiah 29:11). Welcome therefore to a world of answers!

Now, let's briefly touch how the treasures of answers and provisions came about, and can be accessed!

"And, behold, I send the promise of my Father upon you: but tarry ye in the city of Jerusalem, until ye be endued with power from on high." – Luke 24:49.

Having fulfilled all the demands of the law, it's time the promise be delivered. Jesus therefore asked the disciples to wait for the manifestation of this all important promise – the prize He obtained for us!

Remember, with unrighteousness taken out of the way through His sacrifice, righteousness has been ushered in, and the anointing is the final part of the prophecy.

"Seventy weeks are determined upon thy people and upon thy holy city, to finish the transgression, and to make an end of sins, and to make reconciliation for iniquity, and to bring in everlasting righteousness, and to seal up the vision and prophecy, and to anoint the most Holy." – Daniel 9:24.

Many versions of the Bible on the last part of Daniel 9:24, says *"...to anoint the most Holy place."* However, the margin of the Contemporary English Version (CEV) of Daniel 9:24 says, *"... God's Holy One will appear".*

Therefore, whether it's the manifestation of the Holy One of God or Son of God, or the rededication of the temple, which in the New Testament is the Church, the body of Christ, the most important part is that it's time for the Holy Ghost, God's anointing, to take the centre stage!

"Therefore being by the right hand of God exalted, and having received of the Father the promise of the Holy Ghost, he hath shed forth this, which ye now see and hear." – Acts 2:33.

As the Pentecost was being fulfilled, the Holy Ghost came down upon the church of God – sons were born! (Acts 2:1-4). The new man, which after God, is created in righteousness and true holiness came into being! (Ephesians 4:24). What a salvation! The new man is now ready to walk in the ordained good works (Ephesians 2:10).

"Saying with a loud voice, Worthy is the Lamb that was slain to receive power, and riches, and wisdom, and strength, and honour, and glory, and blessing." – Rev. 5:12.

163

Now, that's not the end but a new beginning. The Holy Ghost came as the seal guaranteeing every promise God has ever made! All the promises of God, for which Christ has fulfilled their conditions, are now 'Yes' for every believer! (2Cor. 1:20).

And He is come down to usher the new man into the new creation realities!

"But as it is written, Eye hath not seen, nor ear heard, neither have entered into the heart of man, the things which God hath prepared for them that love him. But God hath revealed them unto us by his Spirit: for the Spirit searcheth all things, yea, the deep things of God.

"For what man knoweth the things of a man, save the spirit of man which is in him? even so the things of God knoweth no man, but the Spirit of God. Now we have received, not the spirit of the world, but the spirit which is of God; that we might know the things that are freely given to us of God... But the natural man receiveth not the things of the Spirit of God: for they are foolishness unto him: neither can he know them, because they are spiritually discerned." – ICor. 2:9-12, 14.

Henceforth, therefore, your life shall never lack taste nor lose colour anymore! Welcome to a world of endless exploration and exploits! May your life, by the Holy Ghost therefore, become a living testimony to all that redemption in Christ affords! (Acts 1:8).

CHAPTER EIGHT

Fearful &
Wonderful Creation!

"The greatest negative in the universe is the Cross for with it God wiped out everything that was not of Himself.

The greatest positive in the universe is the resurrection, for through it God brought into being all!"

– Watchman Nee

The Peculiar Man

"For whom he did foreknow, he also did predestinate to be conformed to the image of his Son, that he might be the firstborn among many brethren."
- Romans 8:29.

> *"Oh yes, you shaped me first inside, then out; You formed me in my mother's womb. I thank you, High God –you're breathtaking! Body and soul, I am marvelously made!"*
> *– Psalm 139:13 (MSG -The Message Bible)*

As we near the conclusion of the Treasures of Redemption, let's dwell briefly on the preciousness of the new man who came out of the waters (at Jordan). Let's look at certain things about this man because until we see the image of this man, which is after Christ, there is no way we can become what God destined us to be!

Remember, those who God did foreknew, He did predestined to be conformed to the image of His Son, which if we know and see in His word, will make it easier for the Holy Spirit to transform us! You are to made to be like the Son!

"But we all, with open face beholding as in a glass the glory of the Lord, are changed into the same image from glory to glory, even as by the Spirit of the Lord."- 2Cor. 3:18.

The Treasure and The Pearl

Again, the kingdom of heaven is like unto a merchant man, seeking goodly pearls: Who, when he had found one pearl of

166

great price, went and sold all that he had, and bought it."
–Matthew 13:44-46.

In two of His short parables of the Kingdom, the Lord Jesus mentioned the purchase of a field in order to secure a treasure buried therein and the purchase of pearl of great value by a merchant man. In both cases, the precious elements are things buried deep in the earth or waters. They also go through a lot of refinement in order to become precious stones. So, treasures and pearls in both parables are not found on the surface but in the deep.

Pearls are precious stones found in the shells of oysters, in the deep waters and their value is based on the account of their beauty and because they are rare.

Your life is truly precious to the Lord for Him to have offered Himself willingly in order to deliver you from sin and death. If nothing was too much for Him to give up for you, how much are you willing to give up for Him?

As we also have seen that the three days and three nights of Jesus in the belly of the earth is actually in the deep waters under the earth. These parable points to Him going therein to bring forth precious souls as "treasures" and "pearls" – just as God had designated Israel as His peculiar treasure!

"Now therefore, if ye will obey my voice indeed, and keep my covenant, then ye shall be a peculiar treasure unto me above all people: for all the earth is mine."- Exodus 19:5.

"For the LORD hath chosen Jacob unto himself, and Israel for his peculiar treasure."- Psalm 135:4.

As we see in the Old Testament priesthood order, there are two items that the high priest wears in order to bear the names of the tribes of Israel before the LORD always. These two items are the Ephod and the Breastplate.

The Ephod hangs upon the shoulders of the high priest signifying his responsibilities before the Lord for them, and the bearing of the names on the breastplate on his chest signifies him carrying them in his heart before the Lord always.

- The Ephod: *"And they shall make the ephod of gold, of blue, and of purple, of scarlet, and fine twined linen, with cunning work. It shall have the two shoulderpieces thereof joined at the two edges thereof; and so it shall be joined together.*

  And thou shalt take two onyx stones, and grave on them the names of the children of Israel: Six of their names on one stone, and the other six names of the rest on the other stone, according to their birth.

  With the work of an engraver in stone, like the engravings of a signet, shalt thou engrave the two stones with the names of the children of Israel: thou shalt make them to be set in ouches of gold.

  And thou shalt put the two stones upon the shoulders of the ephod for stones of memorial unto the children of Israel: and Aaron shall bear their names before the LORD upon his two shoulders for a memorial."
  –Exodus 28:6-7, 9-12.

- The Breastplate: *"And thou shalt make the breastplate of judgment with cunning work; after the work of the ephod thou shalt make it; of gold, of blue, and of purple, and of scarlet, and of fine twined linen, shalt thou make it. Foursquare it shall be being doubled; a span shall be the length thereof, and a span shall be the breadth thereof.*

  And thou shalt set in it settings of stones, even four rows of stones: the first row shall be a sardius, a topaz, and a carbuncle: this shall be the first row. And the second row shall be an emerald, a sapphire, and a diamond. And the third row a ligure, an agate, and an amethyst. And the fourth row a beryl, and an onyx, and a jasper: they shall be set in gold in their inclosings.

  And the stones shall be with the names of the children of Israel, twelve, according to their names, like the engravings of a signet; every one with his name shall they be according to the twelve tribes.

  And Aaron shall bear the names of the children of Israel in the breastplate of judgment upon his heart, when he goeth in unto the holy place, for a memorial before the LORD continually."
  – Exodus 28:15-21, 29.

Indeed, according to the eternal counsel of God, the government of our lives is upon the shoulder of the Lord Jesus Christ and we are engraved in His heart! Beloved, God thinks on and about you daily, moment on moment! Is it any wonder it is written: What is man that thou out mindful of him... that thou shouldest set thine heart upon him"
-Psalm 8:4, Job 7:17.

169

Uncommon Workmanship

The gem stones engraved with the names were the work of men specially picked out by the Lord endowed with uncommon wisdom to work out all that was given to Moses. This prophetically speaks of the uncommon wisdom of God behind the making of the new man in Christ Jesus!

"And the LORD spake unto Moses, saying, See, I have called by name Bezaleel the son of Uri, the son of Hur, of the tribe of Judah: And I have filled him with the spirit of God, in wisdom, and in understanding, and in knowledge, and in all manner of workmanship, To devise cunning works, to work in gold, and in silver, and in brass, And in cutting of stones, to set them, and in carving of timber, to work in all manner of workmanship.

And I, behold, I have given with him Aholiab, the son of Ahisamach, of the tribe of Dan: and in the hearts of all that are wise hearted I have put wisdom, that they may make all that I have commanded thee." – Exodus 31:1-6.

These things are being brought to the fore so you may see and appreciate the peculiarity of the new man, and that the wisdom behind his making is not a common wisdom. A born again Christian is fearfully and wonderfully made by God in Christ.

"For we are his workmanship, created in Christ Jesus unto good works, which God hath before ordained that we should walk in them." - Ephesians 2:10.

You are a workmanship of the living God, specially crafted to show forth His glory!

Fearful & Wonderful Creation!

"How precious also are thy thoughts unto me, O God! how great is the sum of them! If I should count them, they are more in number than the sand..." – Psalm 139:17-18.

We cannot fully exhaust all the works the Lord wrought within the three days and three nights He spent in the heart of the earth. However, He has revealed some which are enough to revolutionize our faith and lives!

Christ's going down into the waters of Jordan was for a comprehensive work that will take eternity to exhaust.

We have mentioned that **Jordan stood both for the grave and the womb. It's the place where an end comes to certain things and new things spring forth.** Jordan represents the cross and the grave where the flesh is laid down and the Spirit takes over. The cross is the line satan cannot cross over!

Now, we need to consider one scripture in the Psalms that points to the lower parts of earth as a womb out of which a new man was born of God!

As you know too well by now, when Jesus went down into the heart of the earth, part of God's work through Him was the creation of a new man and the subsequent emergence of the same God-made man out of the waters!

Consider this Psalm,

"For thou hast possessed my reins: thou hast covered me in my mother's womb. I will praise thee; for I am fearfully and wonderfully made: marvellous are thy works; and that my soul knoweth right well.

My substance was not hid from thee, when <u>I was made in secret, and curiously wrought in the lowest parts of the earth.</u> Thine eyes did see my substance, yet being unperfect; and in thy book all my members were written, which in continuance were fashioned, when as yet there was none of them."
– Psalm 139:12-16.

From this prophetic Psalm, we see that the 'l**ower parts of the earth"** is likened, metaphorically to **"the womb of a woman"**, where the Psalmist says he was being curiously put together by the Creator and Author of life!

The Hebrew word **"qanah"** translated **"possessed"** in this scripture means erect, and by implication to create. It also means to procure or purchase and by implication to own! With this word alone, you can see redemption is at the heart of this new creation!

It's the same word used in Proverbs 8:22 when wisdom personified was declaring that the Lord set Him up in the beginning of His way - before His works of old, before the mountains or anything at all was brought forth!

"The LORD possessed me in the beginning of his way, before his works of old. I was set up from everlasting, from the beginning, or ever the earth was."
– Proverbs 8:22-23.

172

From this scripture, we see the new man created, in Christ Jesus through redemption, **is a product of the unsearchable wisdom of the Living God!** He is not what the natural man can understand! The makeup of this new man is beyond the wisdom of this world! God went to the past, before any was, to setup new foundations for you!

As Bezaleel and Aholiab, among others, were specially endowed with wisdom by God for the works of the tabernacle, the wisdom behind your life as a new man is not of this world!

Truly, you are fearfully and wonderfully made in Christ Jesus!

"Behold, what manner of love the Father hath bestowed upon us, that we should be called the sons of God: therefore the world knoweth us not, because it knew him not." – I John 3:1.

His wisdom is beyond this realm, so be careful not to lower yourself to the level God didn't make you to be. You are not subject to test tube results of men! You are wired up by the everlasting fingers of His Majesty and that's why at times, doctors cannot figure out your being! So, don't let their reports determine your destiny!

While you are not carrying yourself about in pride, be proud and very appreciative of the special, marvelous works God has wrought upon your life in and through the Lord Jesus Christ.

You are indeed a peculiar being, **crafted by the only wise God!**

Full Health Package

Health is wealth Beloved! Therefore let's just mention something briefly about that here. Consider this scripture as touching your redemption in Christ:

"Thine eyes did see my substance, yet being unperfect; and in thy book all my members were written, which in continuance were fashioned, when as yet there was none of them."
– Psalm 139:16.

Now this scripture makes it so clear that your body parts are written in His book, even when as yet there was none of them. We can look briefly at two things here.

Firstly, what body part is missing in your system? Even if it's not yet there, it has been written down! Everything it takes to make your body and life complete, redemption has secured for you! Your fallopian tube, ovary, eggs, sperm cells, brand new heart, eyes, toes... all are written even before they manifest!

They are yours to see that you possess your possession! All things are yours the scripture says! (ICor. 3:21). Remember, that because your physical eyes can't see them manifest yet never invalidates their reality or existence. Consider ICor. 2:9-10, and receive what's yours!

Even before Jesus came, He knew there was a body prepared and waiting for Him, when as yet it hadn't manifested! (Hebrews 10:5). He therefore came and possessed His possession. Now, it's your turn!

Secondly, whatever is not found written in that book is not permitted in your body! God works with details. He wrote down your body parts even before He began fashioning them. Now, you have every right under redemption to resist and reject what's not written in His book for you!

"But he answered and said, Every plant, which my heavenly Father hath not planted, shall be rooted up." – Matthew 15:13.

Now, according to the Book of Revelation, just as those not found in the Lamb's book of life were cast into the lake of fire, every foreign "body" or thing in your system cannot abide but is destined for fire!

"And I saw the dead, small and great, stand before God; and the books were opened: and another book was opened, which is the book of life: and the dead were judged out of those things which were written in the books, according to their works...

And whosoever was not found written in the book of life was cast into the lake of fire." – Revelation 20:12,15.

Stop tolerating that devil in your body. By redemption, your body deserves soundness of health and not affliction! It's your right, therefore exercise it, and receive your full health package!

Now, included in God's wondrous wisdom works is time element which would be great for us to briefly consider here too!

The Fulfilled Time and Kingdom Rule!

"...Jesus came into Galilee, preaching the gospel of the kingdom of God, and saying, The time is fulfilled, and the kingdom of God is at hand: repent ye, and believe the gospel."
– Mark 1:14-15.

We need to visit Christ's statement about time and Kingdom rule once more. These are the two elements in His Gospel – news about what has happened or accomplished symbolically through His baptism and wilderness encounter!

As stated earlier, the three days and three nights is the deepest, greatest and most important of times in the history of creation. As we saw earlier, it was the gathering of times or periods in the law and prophets that had to be fulfilled. And after His resurrection, time is now embodied in the person of Jesus Christ.

In His death and work of redemption, Jesus went into the past – the bottoms or roots of the mountains to effect corrections – pay for transgressions, sins and iniquity, fulfill the broken Sabbath laws, and then usher in everlasting righteousness. He touched the base, foundation and past. Not only that, the future of creation was also settled. The fruit of His work, contrary to one year forgiveness that the Passover rites of Judaism secures, Christ's sacrifice secured eternity for man!

"Having made known unto us the mystery of his will, according to his good pleasure which he hath purposed in himself: That in the dispensation of the fullness of times he might gather together

176

in one all things in Christ, both which are in heaven, and which are on earth; even in him." – Ephesians 1:9-10.

"Blotting out the handwriting of ordinances that was against us, which was contrary to us, and took it out of the way, nailing it to his cross; And having spoiled principalities and powers, he made a shew of them openly, triumphing over them in it. Let no man therefore judge you in meat, or in drink, or in respect of an holyday, or of the new moon, or of the sabbath days: Which are a shadow of things to come; but the body is of Christ."
– Colossians 2:14-17.

All times have gathered together in Christ Jesus! Day and night are in Him. Times and seasons are in His power. Time and space are gathered together in Him.

The Kingdom – the Sovereign rule is now in His hand! Sovereign implies that He is independent of anything and everything! His Kingdom rules over all – all men, creation and elements! All authority in heaven and on earth are in His power! The permission to make anything happen lies with Him only!

"The LORD hath prepared his throne in the heavens; and his kingdom ruleth over all." – Psalm 103:19.

When He returned to Galilee and began to preach the Gospel – declaring the fruits of what happened or what He had accomplished through the symbolic water baptism, time was no barrier to His works. He dealt with time and distance in His miracles as if they didn't exist. He ruled over nature freely!

And you will see that after His resurrection He declared:

"I am Alpha and Omega, the beginning and the ending, saith **the Lord, which is, and which was, and which is to come,** *the Almighty."* - Revelations 1:8.

These titles refer to His accomplished works as the Lord over all things!

In His miracles, you would see the time and space elements were dealt with decisively as if they never existed!

They never stood as barriers for Him in His works!

- He healed: a man born blind

- a man who had been sick and stagnated for thirty-eight years

- the servant of a Roman centurion from a distance

- the daughter of a man from Carpanum – at a distance of a day's journey from where He was

- He raised: a girl from death – the daughter of Jairus, who had just freshly died

- the son of a widow of Nain who had died and was about to be buried
- Lazarus, who had died, buried and had been in the grave for four days!

After His resurrection, He could enter a house whose doors had been locked tightly. Distance or physical elements were no more a barrier to Him and yet He was flesh and bones not spirit! This was because in His going down into the belly of the earth and in His resurrection, He will fill all things and take preeminence over all things! More so, it pleased the Father that in Him should all fullness of creation dwell! He covers all things and above all things. He is simply unstoppable! What a Saviour!

One more thing, He began through His teachings and parables to inform us of the things to come - the present happenings all over the world, had been clearly mentioned by Him, and He also revealed them to His servants – Apostles Paul and John amongst others.

You are fearfully and wonderfully made after the order of Christ. See yourself in the right light that you may show forth God's glory!

CHAPTER NINE

Joshua & His Fellows!

"God justifies the believer not because of the worthiness of his belief but because of His worthiness who is believed!"

– Richard Hooker

Joshua and The Stone

The new man, fearfully and wonderfully made, has unique attributes such that as Jesus incomparably stood out and stands out among men, so also this new man is made in the same likeness to be a wonder.

> *"The risen life of Jesus is the nourishment and strengthening and blessing and life of a Christian."*
> *-Alexander Maclaren*

There are three accounts in the Old Testament scriptures where we have the cases of the name "Joshua" associated with the "Stone" (standing or setup as a witness or testimony). Two of these accounts have the theme of salvation connected with our discussion on water baptism. It will be great and enlightening to dwell briefly on them.

These three accounts are:

- The crossing of Jordan led by Joshua:
  "And Joshua set up twelve stones in the midst of Jordan, in the place where the feet of the priests which bare the ark of the covenant stood: and they are there unto this day."-Joshua 4:9.

- Restoration of the captured ark by the Philistines back to Israel:
  "And they of Bethshemesh were reaping their wheat harvest in the valley: and they lifted up their eyes, and saw the ark, and rejoiced to see it.

  And the cart came into the field of Joshua, a Bethshemite, and stood there, where there was a great stone: and they clave the wood of the cart, and offered the kine a burnt offering unto the LORD.

And the Levites took down the ark of the LORD, and the coffer that was with it, wherein the jewels of gold were, and put them on the great stone: and the men of Bethshemesh offered burnt offerings and sacrificed sacrifices the same day unto the LORD...

And the golden mice, according to the number of all the cities of the Philistines belonging to the five lords, both of fenced cities, and of country villages, even unto the great stone of Abel, whereon they set down the ark of the LORD: which stone remaineth unto this day in the field of Joshua, the Bethshemite." – I Samuel 16:13-18.

- Joshua the high priest after the return from captivity:
  "Hear now, O Joshua the high priest, thou, and thy fellows that sit before thee: for they are men wondered at: for, behold, I will bring forth my servant the BRANCH. For behold the stone that I have laid before Joshua; upon one stone shall be seven eyes: behold, I will engrave the graving thereof, saith the LORD of hosts, and I will remove the iniquity of that land in one day." - *Zechariah 3:8-9.*

As earlier stated, two of these accounts itemized above vividly point to future things of which Jesus Christ duly fulfilled in His redemption work.

The first of the two accounts we are considering is that of Joshua who led Israel into the Promised Land, who in the course of his assignment erected a heap of stones in the midst of Jordan right where the feet of the priests bearing the ark stood as Israel passed over. This stone stands as a witness and testimony of the things to come (Joshua 4:9).

The second case is that of Joshua the high priest, after the return from the Babylonian captivity (having fulfilled the seventy years of desolation prophesied by prophet Jeremiah –Jeremiah 25:11-12, Jeremiah 29:10). In his case too, there was a stone (a symbol of what is to come) upon which there were seven eyes (Zechariah 3:9).

Now, it is worth being mentioned that God's laid stone (of salvation) in Zion is prophetically connected with the heap of stones in the Jordan river where Jesus was baptized; Also the stone placed before Joshua the high priest upon which there are engravings of God and by which iniquity of the land was removed in one day!

Let's consider first the case of Joshua the high priest.

Joshua and The Men of Wonder

"And the angel of the LORD protested unto Joshua, saying, Thus saith the LORD of host; If thou wilt walk in my ways, and if thou wilt keep my charge, then thou shalt also judge my house, and shalt also keep my courts, and I will give thee places to walk among these that stand by.

Hear now, O Joshua the high priest, thou, and thy fellows that sit before thee: for they are men wondered at: for, behold, I will bring forth my servant the BRANCH." – Zechariah 3:6-8

After seventy years of captivity in Babylon, the period in which the transgressions of the land was to be atoned for, the children of Israel began to return to their land. Now, we have the case of Joshua the high priest and others who were involved in rebuilding the temple and the walls of Jerusalem.

Worthy of first mention is what was said to Joshua and his associates and how it was said to them.

The angel of the Lord **"protested"** unto Joshua the scripture says. The word **"protest"** here implies to duplicate, repeat or reiterate, and by implication to charge or earnestly declare. This is like the case where Jesus often says, *"Verily, verily I say unto you..."*

Now, the angel said something peculiar to Joshua the high priest and his associates. They were being addressed in this scripture as **"men wondered at"**. Other translations of the Bible give us insight into this **"wonder"** about Joshua and his fellows.

"Listen, High Priest Joshua, you and your associates seated before you, who are men symbolic of things to come: I am going to bring my servant the Branch." – Zechariah 3:8 (NIV).

Joshua the high priest and his fellows were men who symbolized things to come.

Joshua therefore is symbolic of the Lord's Branch – the messianic name of our Lord Jesus Christ whom the Father has setup as High Priest over His house or temple. The **"fellows"** of Joshua represent the believers in Christ who serve as priests unto the Lord.

The word **"Fellows"** in this scripture comes from a Hebrew root word **"ra'ah"** which by extension implies **associate, companion, brother, friend.** You will note that in the New Testament these are words that Jesus used in describing His disciples.

By implication this means, these are people who are connected with him in every way. Whatever He is, they are, whatever He does, they do likewise! **Whatever He knows, they know because, by their association with Him, He does not keep anything back from them!** There is a oneness of Joshua and his fellows.

"Henceforth I call you not servants; for the servant knoweth not what his lord doeth: but I have called you <u>friends</u>; for all things that I have heard of my Father I have made known unto you. Ye have not chosen me, but I have chosen you, and ordained you, that ye should go and bring forth fruit, and that your fruit should remain..." – John 15:15-16.

When we see the outcome or the fulfilment of this prophetic setting in the light of the New Testament, then we will fully and truly appreciate it. As fulfilled by Jesus Christ, let's see a few scriptures about Him and the believers:

1.   **Unity and oneness**

        "Herein is our love made perfect, that we may have boldness in the day of judgment: because as he is, so are we in this world." – I John 4:17.

2.   **One Sanctification and Brotherhood**

        "Jesus saith unto her, Mary. She turned herself, and saith unto him, Rabboni; which is to say, Master. Jesus saith unto her, Touch me not; for I am not yet ascended to my Father: but go to <u>my brethren</u> (brothers or family), and say unto them, I ascend unto my Father, and your Father; and to my God, and your God." - John 20:16 (Emphasis added).

185

"For both he that sanctifieth and they who are sanctified are <u>all of one</u>: for which cause he is not ashamed to call them <u>brethren</u>, Saying, I will declare thy name unto my brethren, in the midst of the church will I sing praise unto thee. And again, I will put my trust in him. And again, Behold I and the children which God hath given me."- Hebrews 2:11-13.

3.   The Stone and Lively Stones

"To whom coming, as unto a living stone, disallowed indeed of men, but chosen of God, and precious, Ye also, as lively stones, are built up a spiritual house, an holy priesthood, to offer up spiritual sacrifices, acceptable to God by Jesus Christ." – I Peter 2:4-5.

4.   His Body; Our Body - God's Temple

"Then answered the Jews and said unto him, What sign shewest thou unto us, seeing that thou doest these things?

Jesus answered and said unto them, Destroy this temple, and in three days I will raise it up. Then said the Jews, Forty and six years was this temple in building, and wilt thou rear it up in three days?

But he spake of the temple of his body. When therefore he was risen from the dead, his disciples remembered that he had said this unto them; and they believed the scripture, and the word which Jesus had said."
–John 2:18-22.

"What? know ye not that your body is the temple of the Holy Ghost which is in you, which ye have of God, and ye are not your own?" – ICor. 6:19.

Can you now see the connection? The temple is His body – the church – the body of believers, including you!

The "three days" He mentions in scripture above is the three days and three nights He was going to spend in the belly of the earth, after which He would be raised from the dead. That new body coming out of the waters of Jordan is the new temple – the new man for the habitation of God!

5.   **The High Priest and The Priests**

"Wherefore, holy brethren, partakers of the heavenly calling, consider the Apostle and High Priest of our profession, Christ Jesus; Who was faithful to him that appointed him, as also Moses was faithful in all his house."- Hebrews 3:1-2.

"So also Christ glorified not himself to be made an high priest; but he that said unto him, Thou art my Son, to day have I begotten thee."- Hebrews 5:5.

"Now of the things which we have spoken this is the sum: We have such an high priest, who is set on the right hand of the throne of the Majesty in the heavens; A minister of the sanctuary, and of the true tabernacle, which the Lord pitched, and not man."- Hebrews 8:1-2.

"Ye also, as lively stones, are built up a spiritual house, an holy priesthood, to offer up spiritual sacrifices, acceptable to God by Jesus Christ." – I Peter 2:5.

187

6. **Heirs of God and Joint Heirs**

> *"The Spirit itself beareth witness with our spirit, that we are the children of God: And if children, then heirs; heirs of God, and joint-heirs with Christ; if so be that we suffer with him, that we may be also glorified together."*
> *– Romans 8:16-17.*

7. **Priestly Kings Like Himself**

> *"And they sung a new song, saying, Thou art worthy to take the book, and to open the seals thereof: for thou wast slain, and hast redeemed us to God by thy blood out of every kindred, and tongue, and people, and nation; And hast made us unto our God kings and priests: and we shall reign on the earth." – Revelation 5:19-10.*

8. **Saviour and Saviours**

> *"But upon mount Zion shall be deliverance, and there shall be holiness; and the house of Jacob shall possess their possessions... And saviours shall come up on mount Zion to judge the mount of Esau; and the kingdom shall be the LORD'S."- Obadiah 1:17, 21.*

Why are we emphasizing all these? What has these got to do with baptism? Much in every way beloved!

"... He that is joined unto the Lord is one spirit."- 1 Cor. 6:17
The new man made after the image of Jesus Christ has become heir of God, and joint heir with Christ! Being joint heir imply, being brought into the same "associate" category as He, pertaining to inheritance. We are brought in, not by our works but by the reason of our "association" with Him!

188

"According to the grace of God which is given unto me, as a wise masterbuilder, I have laid the foundation, and another buildeth thereon. But let every man take heed how he buildeth thereupon. For other foundation can no man lay than that is laid, which is Jesus Christ."- 1Cor. 3:10-11.

Beloved, **your new life in Christ is not built on human foundation!** There is a greater foundation upon which you are being raised for a God-designed superstructure! Therefore, your life shall never end small!

Joshua, The Temple and His Fellows

"And the word of the LORD came unto me, saying, Take of them of the captivity, even of Heldai, of Tobijah, and of Jedaiah, which are come from Babylon, and come thou the same day, and go into the house of Josiah the son of Zephaniah;

Then take silver and gold, and make crowns, and set them upon the head of Joshua the son of Josedech, the high priest;

And speak unto him, saying, Thus speaketh the LORD of hosts, saying, Behold the man whose name is The BRANCH; and he shall grow up out of his place, and he shall build the temple of the LORD: Even he shall build the temple of the LORD; and he shall bear the glory, and shall sit and rule upon his throne; and he shall be a priest upon his throne: and the counsel of peace shall be between them both." – Zechariah 6:9-13.

Joshua, standing in a prophetic position of our Lord Jesus Christ, was promised by God that he would judge His house and keep His courts if he fully obeyed His rule and walk in His ways (Zechariah 3:7).

189

As stated in the quoted scripture above, Joshua the high priest was also going to:

- ✍ build the temple,
- ✍ bear the glory of the house,
- ✍ he shall sit and rule upon his throne and
- ✍ he shall be a priest upon his throne.

All these points to what Christ has fulfilled. Now, let's summarize all these fulfilments with scriptures:

- ✍ The stone upon which the new temple will be built is the revelation of Himself:

  "He saith unto them, But whom say ye that I am? And Simon Peter answered and said, Thou art the Christ, the Son of the living God. And Jesus answered and said unto him, Blessed art thou, Simon Barjona: for flesh and blood hath not revealed it unto thee, but my Father which is in heaven.

  And I say also unto thee, That thou art Peter, and upon this rock I will build my church; and the gates of hell shall not prevail against it." – Matthew 16:15-18.

  From this scripture, it's crystal clear that Peter was not the rock or stone upon which He is building His church, temple or house! The rock upon which He is building His church, body or house is the revelation of Himself not another man!

Though as Him, we also are lively stones, but not the main foundation. Jesus Christ is the main and sure foundation-God's precious corner stone upon which He builds everything!

✍ He shall bear the glory

"For the Father judgeth no man, but hath committed all judgment unto the Son: That all men should honour the Son, even as they honour the Father. He that honoureth not the Son honoureth not the Father which hath sent him."-John 5:22.

"But unto the Son he saith, Thy throne, O God, is for ever and ever: a sceptre of righteousness is the sceptre of thy kingdom."- Hebrews 1:8.

✍ Jesus Christ is our High Priest and believers are the priests with Him!

"But ye are a chosen generation, a royal priesthood, an holy nation, a peculiar people; that ye should shew forth the praises of him who hath called you out of darkness into his marvellous light."- 1Peter 2:9

"Wherefore, holy brethren, partakers of the heavenly calling, consider the Apostle and High Priest of our profession, Christ Jesus; Who was faithful to him that appointed him, as also Moses was faithful in all his house. For this man was counted worthy of more glory than Moses, inasmuch as he who hath builded the house hath more honour than the house.

For every house is builded by some man; but he that built all things is God. And Moses verily was faithful in all his house, as a servant, for a testimony of those things which were to be spoken after; But Christ as a son over his own house; whose house are we, if we hold fast the confidence and the rejoicing of the hope firm unto the end." – Hebrews 3:1-6.

✍ He is the King with crowns, we are also made kings!

"And they sung a new song, saying, Thou art worthy to take the book, and to open the seals thereof: for thou wast slain, and hast redeemed us to God by thy blood out of every kindred, and tongue, and people, and nation; And hast made us unto our God kings and priests: and we shall reign on the earth."- Rev. 5:9-10.

"And I saw heaven opened, and behold a white horse; and he that sat upon him was called Faithful and True, and in righteousness he doth judge and make war. His eyes were as a flame of fire, and on his head were many crowns; and he had a name written, that no man knew, but he himself.

And he was clothed with a vesture dipped in blood: and his name is called The Word of God. And the armies which were in heaven followed him upon white horses, clothed in fine linen, white and clean... And he hath on his vesture and on his thigh a name written, KING OF KINGS, AND LORD OF LORDS."
- Revelation 19:11-16.

As the Lord's redeemed, you too have a crown, as a king to reign with Him! Remember, He is the King of kings. And guess who those "kings" are? They are the redeemed of the Lord, you and I! From these scriptures among many, it is very clear that the new man is truly fearfully and wonderfully made. Believers need to see themselves in the right light so that they can live right.

"Beloved, now are we the sons of God, and it doth not yet appear what we shall be: but we know that, when he shall appear, we shall be like him; for we shall see him as he is. And every man that hath this hope in him purifieth himself, even as he is pure."
– I John 3:2-3.

By His knowledge, God says His righteous servant shall justify many! (Isaiah 53:11). If we do not have an adequate knowledge of Him, and not just about Him, we shall have nothing to stand upon! These things are being brought to light that we may have a ground, His ground, to stand upon and thereby not be swept away by the forces of darkness who prey on men due to their ignorance!

"... When He shall appear [manifest to us in revelation], we shall be [changed to be] like Him..." I John 3:2 (emphasis mine).

This scripture isn't just about when Jesus returns in the sky, but when He shall appear or be revealed to us we shall take the same form as He! Many believers look far lesser from what Christ is like because there is no adequate revelation of Him to them!

193

Now, let's do a little rephrasing of that portion of scripture: *"... When He shall appear [to us in revelation], we shall be [changed to become] like Him..."* which tallies with 2 Corinthians 3:18, which says: *"But we all, with open face beholding as in a glass the glory of the Lord, are changed into the same image from glory to glory, even as by the Spirit of the Lord."*

Remember what Jesus said of the Holy Spirit, the Spirit of truth: *"...He shall receive of mine and show it unto you."-John 16:14,15.*

Beloved, as He is, so are we in this world! (I John 4:17). Not when we get to heaven. But right here and now! And in order to come into what we are supposed to be, we are to "see" Him as He is!

One question is that: where, and as He is now, can He fall sick? If your answer about Him is an emphatic "NO!", then as He is, so are you! Therefore sickness can never remain with you or in you (without your permission)! As darkness perishes at the appearance of light, the revelation of Christ terminates darkness!

As He overthrew the seats and tables of moneychangers in His temple (Matthew 21:12, John 2:15), may every strange setup of trading, evil exchanges, feasting and manipulation over your life and home be overturned permanently! As He exercised His right in His house, may your right be restored unto you (Ezekiel 21:27).

Whatever constitutes abomination that makes desolate shall be removed far from you!

194

As a new man, you are designed for a new life —a life altogether different from the previous! Live it!

Submit, Change and Resist!

"I beseech you therefore, brethren, by the mercies of God, that ye present your bodies a living sacrifice, holy, acceptable unto God, which is your reasonable service. And be not conformed to this world: but be ye transformed by the renewing of your mind, that ye may prove what is that good, and acceptable, and perfect, will of God." – Romans 12:1-2.

If we do not know who we are, and whose we are, we shall become something other than what God intends us to be. Efforts have been made to bring to light the image of the new man which you carry so that the world will not fit you into its own mold.

As the scripture says, submit your life and faculties to God as a living sacrifice, and as you get renewed in your mind about what God has done in Christ Jesus for you, you shall be transformed! When you submit to God, then you will have power to resist the devil, and he must just flee from you! If you don't submit to God, you cannot subdue the enemy!

"Submit yourselves therefore to God. Resist the devil, and he will flee from you." – James 4:7.

Now beloved, begin to behold Christ afresh! Whatever you can't see in Jesus Christ as He is right now, reject, resist, renounce out of your life and case, and it will not remain!

Whatever can't subdue, oppress, or destroy Him where He is and as He is right now, that is the same case for you! We are His associates, brethren and joint heirs… Glory!

"…Because I live, ye shall live also."-John 14:19.

CHAPTER TEN

The Saviour & His Saviours

"We shall know nothing about beauty of walk till we come to compare our walk with the walk of Christ on earth."

– G. V. Wigram

The Zion Connection

> "When we were baptised, we took upon us not only the name as Christ, but also the law of obedience"
> -Robert D. Hales

"And saviours shall come up on mount Zion to judge the mount of Esau; and the kingdom shall be the LORD'S." - Obadiah 1:21.

In all our discourse so far, if we do not touch this part of this all important topic, our work would have fallen short of the Lord's expectations, as the Lord is not just merely delivering people, but He is making deliverers out of the delivered!

There is that which is the ultimate part of His plan which every believer, every carrier of His Holy Spirit, must key into.

Now, it should be noted that Jordan wasn't the only place with water or river in Israel where baptism could have been conducted. As we are rightly informed, John carried out his baptism elsewhere where people resorted to him in droves.

"And John also was baptizing in Aenon near to Salim, because there was much water there: and they came, and were baptized." -John 3:23.

Aenon was a place of fountains, therefore much water was there. However, Jordan is a key place in scriptures and holds a central place in prophecy with respect to God's plan of salvation and the Messiah.

Furthermore, remember that the second crossing of great waters by Israel was at Jordan. Here they were baptized, though not directly stated but stemming from the prophetic name of Joshua —Jehovah Saves, they were being baptized figuratively unto the Lord Jesus Christ – whose name also is Yeshua —Jehovah Saves.

We see that in the case of Jordan, the priests were bearing the ark of the covenant - a figure of the presence of Jehovah God —Emmanuel (Jehovah God with us), as they crossed over Jordan into the Promised Land.

Let's look back at Psalm 114, which, informing us about the crossing of the waters, rightly states:

"When Israel went out of Egypt, the house of Jacob from a people of strange language; Judah was his sanctuary, and Israel his dominion. The sea saw it, and fled: Jordan was driven back.

The mountains skipped like rams, and the little hills like lambs. What ailed thee, O thou sea, that thou fleddest? thou Jordan, that thou wast driven back? Ye mountains, that ye skipped like rams; and ye little hills, like lambs?

Tremble, thou earth, **at the presence of the Lord, at the presence of the God of Jacob;** *which turned the rock into a standing water, the flint into a fountain of waters."* – Psalm 114:1-8

What parted the waters? The presence of the Lord, the God of Jacob! And look at a new Testament scripture revealing God's mysterious act:

199

"Therefore if any man be in Christ, he is a new creature: old things are passed away; behold, all things are become new. And all things are of God, who hath reconciled us to himself by Jesus Christ, and hath given to us the ministry of reconciliation; To wit, that God was in Christ, reconciling the world unto himself, not imputing their trespasses unto them; and hath committed unto us the word of reconciliation." – 2Cor. 5:17-19.

And it's vividly clear that coming out of the waters, the Holy Spirit like a dove lighted on Jesus and God's voice became manifest. All these at the same Jordan!

Therefore, Jesus being baptized in Jordan was more than a coincidence, as all scriptures concerning Him must be fulfilled.

"And he said unto them, These are the words which I spake unto you, while I was yet with you, that all things must be fulfilled, which were written in the law of Moses, and in the prophets, and in the psalms, concerning me." – Luke 24:44.

This is being brought to fore because there is what we have mentioned earlier in this book, as written in the Book of Joshua about the crossing of Jordan which we now see connected with salvation and Zion.

Right from the Old Testament prophecies, salvation has always been connected with Zion, and we'd like to see that connection with Jordan.

"Oh that the salvation of Israel were come out of Zion! when the LORD bringeth back the captivity of his people, Jacob shall rejoice, and Israel shall be glad." – Psalm 14:7.

Now, when Israel passed over Jordan, God instructed that stones were to be taken from the spot, right in the midst of Jordan, where the feet of those carrying the ark of the covenant stood. These stones would stand as a landmark testimony for the days to come. These stones, twelve in number, were to be taken by twelve men, one from each tribe and erected outside Jordan.

"And it came to pass, when all the people were clean passed over Jordan, that the LORD spake unto Joshua, saying, Take you twelve men out of the people, out of every tribe a man, And command ye them, saying, Take you hence out of the midst of Jordan, out of the place where the priests' feet stood firm, twelve stones, and ye shall carry them over with you, and leave them in the lodging place, where ye shall lodge this night.

Then Joshua called the twelve men, whom he had prepared of the children of Israel, out of every tribe a man: And Joshua said unto them, Pass over before the ark of the LORD your God into the midst of Jordan, and take ye up every man of you a stone upon his shoulder, according unto the number of the tribes of the children of Israel: That this may be a sign among you, that when your children ask their fathers in time to come, saying, What mean ye by these stones?

Then ye shall answer them, That the waters of Jordan were cut off before the ark of the covenant of the LORD; when it passed over Jordan, the waters of Jordan were cut off: and these stones shall be for a memorial unto the children of Israel for ever. And the children of Israel did so as Joshua commanded... And those twelve stones, which they took out of Jordan, did Joshua pitch in Gilgal." – Joshua 4:1-8, 20.

However, there was another set of stones to be taken as a sign and testimony which God asked Joshua to set up in the midst of Jordan, right where the feet of the priests carrying the ark of the covenant stood. This was to be done by Joshua himself.

"And Joshua set up twelve stones in the midst of Jordan, in the place where the feet of the priests which bare the ark of the covenant stood: and they are there unto this day."
– Joshua 4:9.

These stones became hidden from the eyes of men, for when the waters of Jordan returned after Israel passed over, these stones were covered. However, they are there unto this day, as the scripture said, for a testimony. These stones, set up as a sign, represent Jesus Christ, God's foundation for the new creation!

"Therefore thus saith the Lord GOD, Behold, I lay in Zion for a foundation a stone, a tried stone, a precious corner stone, a sure foundation: he that believeth shall not make haste."
– Isaiah 28:16.

The new man has a foundation, laid by God Himself in His Son, that chief corner stone upon which the new order of creation and men are to be built.

This is the very stone which the builders rejected but God made it the chief Cornerstone.

"Wherefore also it is contained in the scripture, Behold, I lay in Sion a chief corner stone, elect, precious: and he that believeth on

him shall not be confounded. Unto you therefore which believe he is precious: but unto them which be disobedient, the stone which the builders disallowed, the same is made the head of the corner, And a stone of stumbling, and a rock of offence, even to them which stumble at the word, being disobedient: whereunto also they were appointed." – I Peter 2:6-7.

As mentioned earlier, the water baptism in Jordan was indeed a stumbling block to the Pharisees and lawyers. As baptism signified the new beginning in and through our Lord Jesus Christ, it became the stumbling block, a place of offence for the so called learned ones or builders! They rejected God's counsel, stood against Jesus Christ, being disobedient to God and His word!

For in Christ Jesus, the scripture promised, there shall be deliverance and holiness and those in Him will go on to possess their possessions. We find that deliverance and holiness fulfilled according to Daniel 9:24, which we have considered in an earlier section of this book.

"But upon mount Zion shall be deliverance, and there shall be holiness; and the house of Jacob shall possess their possessions."
– Obadiah 1:17.

However, having laid a foundation, which cannot be shaken nor destroyed, God has a building in mind. Beloved, a foundation is a substructure, often hidden from the public view but upon which a building is erected. A foundation therefore, automatically pre-supposes or necessitates a building. So when God laid a foundation in Zion, it's because He had a building in mind. That building is built with living stones.

"Ye also, as lively stones, are built up a spiritual house, an holy priesthood, to offer up spiritual sacrifices, acceptable to God by Jesus Christ." - I Peter 2:5.

"God became man to turn creatures into sons: not simply to produce better men of the old kind but to produce a new kind of man"
-CS Lewis

Delivered to His Deliverers!

"But upon mount Zion shall be deliverance, and there shall be holiness; and the house of Jacob shall possess their possessions." - Obadiah 1:17.

Why have we used this scripture here? First, the word deliverance here is about escape or salvation. Secondly, it's essentially because of what verse twenty-one of the same scripture says regarding God's kingdom programme:

"And saviours shall come up on mount Zion to judge the mount of Esau; and the kingdom shall be the LORD'S." - Obadiah 1:21.

Zion, which pointed to the person of Jesus Christ and became personalized in Him, is the place of not just saving people but the raising of saviours, deliverers who will go and conquer the nations in the strength of their Head and Captain. As in the Old Testament when Israel was ruled by judges, they were referred to as saviours or deliverers as God worked through these vessels.

"Therefore thou deliveredst them into the hand of their enemies, who vexed them: and in the time of their trouble, when they

cried unto thee, thou heardest them from heaven; and according to thy manifold mercies thou gavest them saviours, who saved them out of the hand of their enemies." – Nehemiah 9:27.

You see Beloved, God isn't just interested in saving a few people, but that the earth be filled with the knowledge of His glory.

Remember, part of God's covenant promise to Abraham was that in his seed all the nations of the earth shall be blessed (Genesis 12:3, Genesis 22:17-18). That seed is Christ and He's now sending forth believers as His ambassadors to all the nations.

There are many souls today all over the nations crying out in affliction and agony, and God is raising up deliverers for their sake. You are designed, according to God's Abrahramic Covenant, a blessing to the nations!

It's not enough to sit down and rejoice in the Lord's salvation but to rise up and be His instrument to save others. No matter what the enemy can ever muster, Christ has already defeated him and given us victory.

Yours is to begin to explore and walk in the light of those things the Lord has done, and to become a blessing to others.

"And when he had so said, he shewed unto them his hands and his side. Then were the disciples glad, when they saw the Lord. Then said Jesus to them again, Peace be unto you: as my Father hath sent me, even so send I you." – John 20:20-21.

205

And again He said,

"Go ye therefore, and teach all
nations, baptizing them in the
name of the Father, and of the Son,
and of the Holy Ghost:

> "There are two sides to
> this baptism: The first is
> you possess the Spirit;
> The second is that the
> Spirit possess you".
> - Smith Wigglesworth

*Teaching them to observe all
things whatsoever I have commanded you: and, lo, I am with
you alway, even unto the end of the world. Amen."
– Matthew 28:19-20.*

Therefore, salvation is our entrance into an endless treasure
through which God's end goal of filling the whole creation
with the knowledge of His glory is reached.

Saviours – God's End Goal!

*"The LORD said unto my Lord, Sit thou at my right hand, until
I make thine enemies thy footstool. The LORD shall send the rod
of thy strength out of Zion: rule thou in the midst of thine
enemies." – Psalm 110:1-2.*

It is clear from scriptures that after Christ was raised from the
dead, forty days later, He was taken up to glory where He sent
forth the Holy Ghost. But before then, He had declared:

*"In the last day, that great day of the feast, Jesus stood and cried,
saying, If any man thirst, let him come unto me, and drink. He
that believeth on me, as the scripture hath said, out of his belly
shall flow rivers of living water. (But this spake he of the Spirit,
which they that believe on him should receive: for the Holy
Ghost was not yet given; because that Jesus was not yet
glorified.)" – John 7:37-39*

206

And after His resurrection, the Lord declared:

"But ye shall receive power, after that the Holy Ghost is come upon you: and ye shall be witnesses unto me both in Jerusalem, and in all Judaea, and in Samaria, and unto the uttermost part of the earth." – Acts 1:8.

The Lord has an end-goal, and it is: that the whole creation will be filled with the knowledge of His glory. He therefore sends men, in the power of the Holy Ghost – His saved men – out from Zion to go forth and rule in the midst of His enemies and bring His dominion to bear.

Scriptures call these saved men saviours! – for God is saving others through them! They are not men who live for themselves but vessels in His hands to bring His light and glory to bear all over creation. As His Son, men who were once nothing, he has raised up to become instruments of His salvation unto the ends of the earth!

Water has been used in the metaphoric description of salvation by the Lord (John 4:14) and the Holy Spirit has been likened unto a river that flows from every believer (John 7:37-39). That river, is destined for nations to bring the Lord's salvation unto the ends of the earth.

"He that believeth on me, as the scripture hath said, out of his belly shall flow rivers of living water. (But this spake he of the Spirit, which they that believe on him should receive: for the Holy Ghost was not yet given; because that Jesus was not yet glorified.)" – John 7:38-39.

207

"They shall not hurt nor destroy in all my holy mountain: for the earth shall be full of the knowledge of the LORD, as the waters cover the sea. And in that day there shall be a root of Jesse, which shall stand for an ensign of the people; to it shall the Gentiles seek: and his rest shall be glorious." – Isaiah 11:9-10.

Therefore, every believer is not to sit down and think they are on their way to heaven but to set out to work and take the Lord's glory to the nations.

You are not saved to sit. Only the Lord Jesus Christ, having done all things seats as He watches the fruits of His travail prevail on the earth!

"...He shall see his seed, he shall prolong his days, and the pleasure of the LORD shall prosper in his hand. He shall see of the travail of his soul, and shall be satisfied: by his knowledge shall my righteous servant justify many..." – Isaiah 53:10-11.

You are His chosen seed for the establishment of His reign in all the nations. You are the offspring and fruit of His travail, and as every seed produces after its kind, it's time you set out and walk in His footsteps!

There are men in bondage waiting for your appearance! Their destinies are tied to yours for liberation – the oppressed, addicts, suppressed, the destitute…

"For the earth shall be filled with the knowledge of the glory of the LORD, as the waters cover the sea." – Habakkuk 2:14.

When the Lord said, "Go ye unto all the nations…" (Matthew 28:18), it's because He has made a way for that to happen! He will never send you on a mission where retreat is inevitable and advancement is practically impossible! Never!

"Now thanks be unto God, which always causeth us to triumph in Christ, and maketh manifest the savour of his knowledge by us in every place." – 2Cor. 2:14.

As the true Shepherd, He is always ahead of His sheep. Wherever He sends, His footprints are already ahead. They may be invisible to the naked eyes, but we follow by faith through His voice! He will not send you where he had not gone ahead!

"And when he putteth forth his own sheep, he goeth before them, and the sheep follow him: for they know his voice." – John 10:4.

Even when Israel left Egypt, God knew there was Red sea ahead of them. He had factored in all the challenges before them before they ever set forth. When they got to the sea, He told them to go forward! As you are well aware, the sea opened up by the matchless power of His Majesty!

"Your road led through the sea, your pathway through the mighty waters – a pathway no one knew was there!"
– Psalm 77:19 (NLT).

From your discoveries and encounters through this little book, volumes shall be written on the pages of your own life that will become a light for others! Your mess shall the Lord turn to become a message! Your burdens shall transform to become a blessing! That curse shall no more be a case! It is finished, as declared by the Lord Jesus Christ!

God has sworn that the earth shall be filled with His glory, and you are designed as the carrier, vessel and bearer of the knowledge of that glory! Only the undiscerning will stay out of it! Wise up and plunge into the Lord's unstoppable procession! The gates of hell may set itself on the way, but shall not and cannot prevail!

"But as truly as I live, all the earth shall be filled with the glory of the LORD." - Numbers 14:21.

God has sworn, and will not back out, therefore step out at His beckon!

EPILOGUE

Go & Be A Blessing!

"Let us hear the conclusion of the whole matter: Fear God, and keep his commandments: for this is the whole duty of man.

For God shall bring every work into judgment, with every secret thing, whether it be good, or whether it be evil."

– Ecclesiastes 12:13-14

Live His Life!

"Ye are the light of the world. A city that is set on an hill cannot be hid. Neither do men light a candle, and put it under a bushel, but on a candlestick; and it giveth light unto all that are in the house. Let your light so shine before men, that they may see your good works, and glorify your Father which is in heaven."
– Matthew 5:14-16.

> *Don't shine so others can see you. Shine so that through you, others can see Him!*
> *-Author Unknown*

As stated at the outset of this book, I have not written this so that people may be filled with knowledge but come to light of Jesus Christ's knowledge and become His living epistle written with the Holy Spirit - the Finger of God!

"Ye are our epistle written in our hearts, known and read of all men: Forasmuch as ye are manifestly declared to be the epistle of Christ ministered by us, written not with ink, but with the Spirit of the living God; not in tables of stone, but in fleshy tables of the heart." – 2Cor. 3:2-3.

We thus become, through the ministry of the Holy Spirit, living witnesses of all that God has wrought in Christ. (Acts 1:8)

The Christian life is the most beautiful life! Though fraught with challenges, we have already been made more than conquerors before the journey even began! Christianity is not about living your life but Him living His life in and through you!

212

"I am crucified with Christ: nevertheless I live; yet not I, but Christ liveth in me: and the life which I now live in the flesh I live by the faith of the Son of God..." – Galatians 2:20.

Using the key of water baptism in particular, we have just opened through this book, the world of timeless and endless treasures that redemption in Christ Jesus holds for every man.

Water baptism has pointed us to the immense work of redemption in Christ and the change of citizenship that follows for every believer and receiver of the grace of salvation that is in Him!

> *"Long-lasting victory can never be separated from a long-lasting stand on the foundation of the cross."*
> -Watchman Nee

The few seconds spent under water during baptism gathers together immeasurable blessings of the Lord.

Now, knowledge profits nothing if not effectively engaged. Those who can't read, those who refuse reading and those who don't understand what they read stand in the same category of ignorance! Captivity is the result of such. But light has come for you, therefore engage it!

"And the vision of all is become unto you as the words of a book that is sealed, which men deliver to one that is learned, saying, Read this, I pray thee: and he saith, I cannot; for it is sealed: And the book is delivered to him that is not learned, saying, Read this, I pray thee: and he saith, I am not learned."
– Isaiah 29:11-12.

213

From the light you have encountered so far, the Bible should no more be an unprofitable parable for you but keys to unlocking the Kingdom treasures. Jesus our Lord says,

"For whosoever hath, to him shall be given, and he shall have more abundance: but whosoever hath not, from him shall be taken away even that he hath." – Matthew 13:12.

Therefore, more shall come your way from the understanding so far! Your life is set for the increase if only you will engage what you have gleaned. No more shall the enemy rob you of what is already yours, in Jesus' name!

It has been prayerfully hoped that as people will read through this book, howbeit prayerfully and engage the light of the knowledge of the Lord it has briefly shown, coupled with fasting if so desired, that drastic changes will take place in such lives!

Yours is an enviable heritage, therefore live it! There is a sound of the abundance of rain, praise and testimonies coming from your end! Shalom!

www.ingramcontent.com/pod-product-compliance
Lightning Source LLC
LaVergne TN
LVHW011154080426
835508LV00007B/389